ROYAL COURT

Royal Court Theatre presents

TUSK TUSK

by **Polly Stenham**

First performance at the Royal Court Jerwood Theatre Upstairs, Sloane Square, London on 28 March 2009.

supported by

JERWOOD
NEW PLAYWRIGHT

822.
92
STE

wallace shawn season

ROYAL COURT

the fever

2 April – 2 May

Clare Higgins delivers
Shawn's seminal play.

grasses of a thousand colours

12 May – 13 June

Miranda Richardson and
Wallace Shawn in his
explicit new play.

aunt dan and lemon

20 May – 27 June

Lemon (**Jane Horrocks**) hears
intimate secrets from Dan's
(**Lorraine Ashbourne**) exotic
adult world.

There will also be readings of the plays The Hotel Play, Our Late Night, A
Thought in Three Parts, Marie and Bruce and The Designated Mourner, as well
as screenings of the films My Dinner with André and Vanya on 42nd Street.

020 7565 5000
www.royalcourttheatre.com

ARTS COUNCIL ENGLAND

TUSK TUSK

by **Polly Stenham**

Cast in order of appearance
Eliot **Toby Regbo**
Maggie **Bel Powley**
Finn **Finn Bennett, Austin Moulton**
Cassie **Georgia Groome**
Katie **Caroline Harker**
Roland **Tom Beard**

Director **Jeremy Herrin**
Designer **Robert Innes Hopkins**
Lighting Designer **Neil Austin**
Sound Designer **Emma Laxton**
Casting Director **Amy Ball**
Assistant Director **Natalie Ibu**
Production Manager **Tariq Rifaat**
Stage Managers **Joni Carter, Bonnie Morris**
Costume Supervisor **Jackie Orton**
Fight Director **Renny Krupinski**
Stage Management Work Placement **Jessica Harwood**
Set Built by **RCT Stage Department**

The Royal Court and Stage Management would like to thank the following for their help with this production: Barnet Recycling Centre, Paul Foster, MDF The BiPolar Organisation, Natalie Miles, The People Show, Rethink, Jonathan Williams (Royal Borough of Kensington & Chelsea), Dawn Willis.

THE COMPANY

POLLY STENHAM (Writer)

THE ROYAL COURT: That Face (& Duke of York's).

OTHER THEATRE INCLUDES: Hotel California (Latitude).

AWARDS INCLUDE: 2008 Critics' Circle Award for Most Promising Playwright, 2007 Evening Standard Award for Most Promising Playwright, 2007 Best New Play TMA for That Face.

After the success of That Face, Polly was awarded one of the UK Film Council's first grants from their newly structured development fund and is being mentored by Pawel Pawlikowski to adapt her play into a feature film.

NEIL AUSTIN (Lighting Designer)

FOR THE ROYAL COURT: Flesh Wound, Trust.

OTHER THEATRE INCLUDES: England People Very Nice, Mrs Affleck, Oedipus, Her Naked Skin, Afterlife, The Emperor Jones, Philistines, The Man of Mode, Thérèse Raquin, The Seafarer, Henry IV Parts 1 & 2, Fix Up, The Night Season, A Prayer for Owen Meany, The Walls, Further than the Furthest Thing (National); Twelfth Night, Piaf, Parade, John Gabriel Borkman, Don Juan in Soho, The Cryptogram, Frost/Nixon, The Wild Duck, The Cosmonaut's Last Message to the Woman He Once Loved in the Former Soviet Union, Henry IV, World Music, After Miss Julie, Caligula (Donmar); King Lear, The Seagull, Much Ado About Nothing, Romeo & Juliet, King John, Julius Caesar, Two Gentleman of Verona (RSC); The Homecoming, Marianne Dreams, Dying for it, Tom & Viv, Romance, Macbeth (Almeida); No Man's Land (Duke of York's); Dealer's Choice (Trafalgar Studios); A Life in the Theatre (Apollo); Japes (Haymarket).

DANCE INCLUDES: Rhapsody (Royal Ballet), The Soldier's Tale (ROH2), The Canterville Ghost (ENB), Pineapple Poll (Birmingham Royal Ballet), Darkness & Light (Tokyo).

AWARDS INCLUDE: 2008 Knight of Illumination Award for Parade

TOM BEARD (Roland)

THEATRE INCLUDES: For Services Rendered (Newbury Watermill); Private Lives (Ipswich); The Holy Terror (Duke of York's); Three Sisters (Playhouse Theatre) The Tempest, Pericles, Henry VI Parts 1,2 & 3 (RSC); Macbeth (Sheffield Crucible); Hamlet (Gielgud); She Stoops to Conquer (Queen's Theatre); Becket (Haymarket Theatre).

TELEVISION INCLUDES: Kingdom, Wallander, Ten Days to War, Midsomer Murders, George Gently, The Fixer, The Whistleblowers, Clapham Junction. Silent Witness, Party Animals, Spooks, Robin Hood, Six Degrees of Francis Bacon, The Government Inspector, Rosemary & Thyme, Holby City, Murder City, EastEnders, In Defence, Poirot, Wing & A Prayer, Aristocrats, Staying Alive (series 1 & II), The Investigator, McCallum, Ain't Misbehavin', Soldier Solder, Peak Practice, Harnessing Peacocks, Unnatural Pursuits, Boon, Jewels, Heartbeat, Bad Girl.

FILM INCLUDES: Vanity Fair.

FINN BENNETT (Finn)

THEATRE INCLUDES: A Christmas Carol (King's Head).

GEORGIA GROOME (Cassie)

Tusk Tusk is Georgia's professional stage debut.

FILM INCLUDES: Leaving Eva, Angus, Thongs and Perfect Snogging, The Disappeared, The Cottage, My Mother, London to Brighton.

CAROLINE HARKER (Katie)

FOR THE ROYAL COURT: The Strip, Editing Process.

OTHER THEATRE INCLUDES: All Mouth (Menier Chocolate Factory); Entertaining Angels (Chichester Festival Theatre); Present Laughter (No 1 Tour); Battle Royal (National); Falling (Hampstead); Things We Do for Love (West End); Life Goes On (Basingstoke Theatre); A Mongrel's Heart (Royal Lyceum Theatre); Hidden Laughter (UK Tour); Sweet Charity, Daisy Pulls It Off, Don Juan (Harrogate Theatre).

TELEVISION INCLUDES: The Commander, The Man Who Lost His Head, Margaret, Murder in Suburbia, Foyle's War, Auf Wiedersehen Pet, Hans Christian Anderson, I Saw You, Armadillo, Keeping Mum, A Touch of Frost, Kavanagh QC, Casualty, A Dance to the Music of Time, Holding On, Moll Flanders, Harry Enfield & Chums, Honey for Tea, Middlemarch, Covington Cross, Riders, Growing Rich, Chancer, Midsomer Murders.

FILM INCLUDES: A Woman of the North, The Madness of King George.

RADIO INCLUDES: Snobs, If I Should Go Away, Westwood, Mrs Henderson's Christmas Party, Best Foot Forward, The Golden Pavements, The Swish of the Curtain, Still Life.

JEREMY HERRIN (Director)

FOR THE ROYAL COURT: The Vertical Hour, That Face (& Duke of York's).

OTHER THEATRE AS DIRECTOR INCLUDES: Marble (Abbey, Dublin); A Family Reunion (Donmar); Sudden Collapses in Public Places (Sage, Gateshead/Live Theatre); Gathered Dust and Dead Skin, The Lovers, Our Kind of Fun, Toast, Dirty Nets, Smack Family Robinson, Attachments, From the Underworld (Live Theatre); The Last Post (tour/Live Theatre); Personal Belongings (Edinburgh Festival/Live Theatre); ne1 (Theatre Royal, Newcastle/Live Theatre); Knives in Hens (Live Theatre/Northumbria Academy).

FOR THE ROYAL COURT, AS ASSISTANT DIRECTOR: My Night with Reg, Babies, Thyestes, The Kitchen.

FILM & TELEVISION INCLUDES: The Inventor, Linked, Dead Terry, Warmth, Cold Calling.

Jeremy is an Associate Director at the Royal Court.

ROBERT INNES HOPKINS (Designer)

FOR THE ROYAL COURT: The Pain and the Itch, Redundant.

RECENT THEATRE INCLUDES: Marble (Abbey, Dublin); Dallas Sweetman (Canterbury Cathedral); Romeo & Juliet, Twelfth Night (Open Air Theatre, Regent's Park); The Member of the Wedding (Young Vic);Our Country's Good (Liverpool Playhouse); Carousel (Chichester Festival Theatre).

OPERA INCLUDES: Rape of Lucretia (Snape Maltings); Billy Budd (Santa Fe Opera); Carmen (Bolshoi); Lohengrin (Geneva Opera) Rigoletto (Lyric Opera, Chicago); Betrothal in a Monastery (Glyndebourne); Die Soldaten (Ruhr Triennale/Lincoln Center Festival.

AWARDS INCLUDE: Opernwelt Set Designer of the Year 2007 for Die Soldaten.

NATALIE IBU (Assistant Director)

AS ASSISTANT DIRECTOR FOR THE ROYAL COURT: Seven Jewish Children, Wig Out!, The Girlfriend Experience.

AS DIRECTOR, THEATRE INCLUDES: Starlings, God & All That, Cocks & Robbers, Ashes, What's Lost (readings, Royal Court); The Red Shoes Re-heeled (Royal Lyceum Youth Theatre, Edinburgh); We Were... Re-imagining the Mother (G12, Glasgow); We Were... In Development (Citizens', Glasgow); We Were... In a Cafe (Gramofon, Glasgow); Say What… (Arches Scratch, Glasgow); I Know All The Secrets In My World… (Contact, Manchester); Women's Voices (NewWriting NewWorlds, Glasgow); Hang Up, Lesson Learned (Citizens' Young Company, Glasgow); Blooded (Fresh Perspectives, Mansfield); Road (De Montfort Univsersity, Leicester).

AS ASSISTANT DIRECTOR, THEATRE INCLUDES: Zameen (Kali Theatre, London); Fugee (Royal Lyceum Youth Theatre, Edinburgh); Peter Pan, Desire Under the Elms (Citizens', Glasgow); The Shadow of a Pie (Lung Ha's Theatre Company, Edinburgh); The Ghost Downstairs, The Butterfly Lion (New Perspectives Theatre Company, East Midlands).

Natalie is Trainee Director at the Royal Court, supported by ITV under the ITV Theatre Director Scheme.

EMMA LAXTON (Sound Designer)

FOR THE ROYAL COURT: Faces in the Crowd, That Face (& Duke of York's), Gone Too Far!, Catch, Scenes From The Back Of Beyond, Woman and Scarecrow, The World's Biggest Diamond, Incomplete & Random Acts of Kindness, My Name is Rachel Corrie (& Playhouse/Minetta Lane, New York/Galway Festival/Edinburgh Festival), Bone, The Weather, Bear Hug, Terrorism, Food Chain.

OTHER THEATRE INCLUDES: Wrecks, Broken Space Season, 2000 Feet Away, Tinderbox (Bush); Treasure Island (Theatre Royal Haymarket); A Chistmas Carol (Chichester Festival Theatre); Welcome to Ramallah (iceandfire); Pornography (Birmingham Rep/Traverse); Shoot/Get Treasure/Repeat (National); Europe (Dundee Rep/Barbican Pit); Other Hands (Soho); The Unthinkable (Sheffield Crucible); My Dad's a Birdman (Young Vic); The Gods Are Not To Blame (Arcola); Late Fragment (Tristan Bates).

AUSTIN MOULTON (Finn)

THEATRE INCLUDES: Fiddler on the Roof (UK Tour); Joseph and his Amazing Technicolour Dreamcoat (Bill Kenwright).

OPERA INCLUDES: Le Bohème, Aida (Ellen Kent Productions).

BEL POWLEY (Maggie)

Tusk Tusk is Bel's professional stage debut.

TELEVISION INCLUDES: Little Dorrit, The Bill, MI High Series I & II, Whistleblowers.

TOBY REGBO (Eliot)

Tusk Tusk is Toby's professional stage debut.

TELEVISION INCLUDES: MI High, Sharpe's Challenge.

FILM INCLUDES: Mr Nobody, 1939.

THE ENGLISH STAGE COMPANY
AT THE ROYAL COURT

*'For me the theatre is really a religion or way of life.
You must decide what you feel the world is about and
what you want to say about it, so that everything in
the theatre you work in is saying the same thing ...
A theatre must have a recognisable attitude. It will
have one, whether you like it or not.'*

George Devine, first artistic director of the
English Stage Company: notes for an unwritten
book.

photo: Stephen Cummiskey

As Britain's leading national company dedicated to new work, the Royal Court Theatre produces new plays
of the highest quality, working with writers from all backgrounds, and addressing the problems and
possibilities of our time.

"The Royal Court has been at the centre of British cultural life for the past 50 years, an engine room for
new writing and constantly transforming the theatrical culture." Stephen Daldry

Since its foundation in 1956, the Royal Court has presented premieres by almost every leading
contemporary British playwright, from John Osborne's Look Back in Anger to Caryl Churchill's A Number
and Tom Stoppard's Rock 'n' Roll. Just some of the other writers to have chosen the Royal Court to
premiere their work include Edward Albee, John Arden, Richard Bean, Samuel Beckett, Edward Bond,
Leo Butler, Jez Butterworth, Martin Crimp, Ariel Dorfman, Stella Feehily, Christopher Hampton, David Hare,
Eugène Ionesco, Ann Jellicoe, Terry Johnson, Sarah Kane, David Mamet, Martin McDonagh, Conor McPherson,
Joe Penhall, Mark Ravenhill, Simon Stephens, Wole Soyinka, Polly Stenham, David Storey, Debbie Tucker
Green, Arnold Wesker and Roy Williams.

"It is risky to miss a production there." Financial Times

In addition to its full-scale productions, the Royal Court also facilitates international work at a grass roots
level, developing exchanges which bring young writers to Britain and sending British writers, actors and
directors to work with artists around the world. The research and play development arm of the Royal Court
Theatre, The Studio, finds the most exciting and diverse range of new voices in the UK. The Studio runs play-
writing groups including the Young Writers Programme, Critical Mass for black, Asian and minority ethnic
writers and the biennial Young Writers Festival. For further information, go to
www.royalcourttheatre.com/ywp.

"Yes, the Royal Court is on a roll. Yes, Dominic Cooke has just the genius and kick that this venue needs...
It's fist-bitingly exciting." Independent

JERWOOD
NEW PLAYWRIGHTS

Since 1994 Jerwood New Playwrights has contributed to 54 new plays at the Royal Court including Joe Penhall's SOME VOICES, Mark Ravenhill's SHOPPING AND FUCKING (co-production with Out of Joint), Ayub Khan Din's EAST IS EAST (co-production with Tamasha), Martin McDonagh's THE BEAUTY QUEEN OF LEENANE (co-production with Druid Theatre Company), Conor McPherson's THE WEIR, Nick Grosso's REAL CLASSY AFFAIR, Sarah Kane's 4.48 PSYCHOSIS, Gary Mitchell's THE FORCE OF CHANGE, David Eldridge's UNDER THE BLUE SKY, David Harrower's PRESENCE, Simon Stephens' HERONS, Roy Williams' CLUBLAND, Leo Butler's REDUNDANT, Michael Wynne's THE PEOPLE ARE FRIENDLY, David Greig's OUTLYING ISLANDS, Zinnie Harris' NIGHTINGALE AND CHASE, Grae Cleugh's FUCKING GAMES, Rona Munro's IRON, Richard Bean's UNDER THE WHALEBACK, Ché Walker's FLESH WOUND, Roy Williams' FALLOUT, Mick Mahoney's FOOD CHAIN, Ayub Khan Din's NOTES ON FALLING LEAVES, Leo Butler's LUCKY DOG, Simon Stephens' COUNTRY MUSIC, Laura Wade's BREATHING CORPSES, Debbie Tucker Green's STONING MARY, David Eldridge's INCOMPLETE AND RANDOM ACTS OF KINDNESS, Gregory Burke's ON TOUR, Stella Feehily's O GO MY MAN, Simon Stephens' MOTORTOWN, Simon Farquhar's RAINBOW KISS, April de Angelis, Stella Feehily, Tanika Gupta, Chloe Moss and Laura Wade's CATCH, Mike Bartlett's MY CHILD and Polly Stenham's THAT FACE.

In 2008 Jerwood New Playwrights supported THE PRIDE by Alexi Kaye Campbell, SCARBOROUGH by Fiona Evans, OXFORD STREET by Levi David Addai and GONE TOO FAR! by Bola Agbaje. In 2009 Jerwood New Playwrights supported SHADES by Alia Bano.

Jerwood Charitable Foundation is a registered charity dedicated to imaginative and responsible funding of the arts and other areas of human endeavour and excellence.

Levi David Addai's OXFORD STREET
(photo: Tristram Kenton)

Alexi Kaye Campbell's THE PRIDE
(photo: Stephen Cummisky)

PROGRAMME SUPPORTERS

The Royal Court (English Stage Company Ltd) receives its principal funding from Arts Council England, London. It is also supported financially by a wide range of private companies, charitable and public bodies, and earns the remainder of its income from the box office and its own trading activities.

The Genesis Foundation supports the Royal Court's work with International Playwrights.

The Jerwood Charitable Foundation supports new plays by new playwrights through the Jerwood New Playwrights series.

The Artistic Director's Chair is supported by a lead grant from The Peter Jay Sharp Foundation, contributing to the activities of the Artistic Director's office. Over the past ten years the BBC has supported the Gerald Chapman Fund for directors.

ROYAL COURT DEVELOPMENT ADVOCATES
John Ayton
Elizabeth Bandeen
Tim Blythe
Anthony Burton
Sindy Caplan
Cas Donald
Allie Esiri
Celeste Fenichel
Stephen Marquardt
Emma Marsh (Vice Chair)
Mark Robinson
William Russell (Chair)
Deborah Shaw Marquardt
Daniel Winterfeldt

PUBLIC FUNDING
Arts Council England, London
British Council

CHARITABLE DONATIONS
American Friends of the Royal Court Theatre
Anthony Burton
Gerald Chapman Fund
Columbia Foundation
The Sidney & Elizabeth Corob Charitable Trust
Credit Suisse First Boston Foundation*
Cowley Charitable Trust
The Edmond de Rothschild Foundation*
Do Well Foundation Ltd*
The D'Oyly Carte Charitable Trust
Esmée Fairbairn Foundation
Francis Finlay*
Frederick Loewe Foundation*
Genesis Foundation
Haberdashers' Company
Jerwood Charitable Foundation
John Thaw Foundation
Kudos Film and Televisoin
Lynn Foundation
John Lyon's Charity

The Laura Pels Foundation*
The Martin Bowley Charitable Trust
The Patchwork Charitable Foundation*
Paul Hamlyn Foundation
Jerome Robbins Foundation*
Rose Foundation
Royal College of Psychiatrists
The Peter Jay Sharp Foundation*
Sobell Foundation

CORPORATE SUPPORTERS & SPONSORS
BBC
Hugo Boss

BUSINESS BENEFACTORS & MEMBERS
Grey London
Lazard
Merrill Lynch
Vanity Fair

INDIVIDUAL SUPPORTERS

ICE-BREAKERS
Act IV
Anonymous
Ossi and Paul Burger
Mrs Helena Butler
Cynthia Corbett
Shantelle David
Charlotte & Nick Fraser
Mark & Rebecca Goldbart
Linda Grosse
Mr & Mrs Tim Harvey-Samuel
The David Hyman Charitable Trust
David Lanch
Colette & Peter Levy
Watcyn Lewis
David Marks
Nicola McFarland
Janet & Michael Orr

Pauline Pinder
Mr & Mrs William Poeton
The Really Useful Group
Lois Sieff OBE
Gail Steele
Nick & Louise Steidl

GROUND-BREAKERS
Anonymous
Moira Andreae
Jane Attias*
Elizabeth & Adam Bandeen
Philip Blackwell
Mrs D H Brett
Sindy & Jonathan Caplan
Mr & Mrs Gavin Casey
Carole & Neville Conrad
Clyde Cooper
Andrew & Amanda Cryer
Robyn M Durie
Hugo Eddis
Mrs Margaret Exley CBE
Robert & Sarah Fairbairn
Celeste & Peter Fenichel
Andrew & Jane Fenwick
Ginny Finegold
Wendy Fisher
Hugh & Henri Fitzwilliam-Lay
Joachim Fleury
John Garfield
Lydia & Manfred Gorvy
Richard & Marcia Grand*
Nick & Catherine Hanbury-Williams
Sam & Caroline Haubold
Nicholas Josefowitz
David P Kaskel &
Christopher A Teano
Peter & Maria Kellner*
Mrs Joan Kingsley &
Mr Philip Kingsley
Mr & Mrs Pawel Kisielewski
Varian Ayers and Gary Knisely
Rosemary Leith
Kathryn Ludlow
Emma Marsh
Barbara Minto
Gavin & Ann Neath
William Plapinger & Cassie Murray*

Mark Robinson
Paul & Jill Ruddock
William & Hilary Russell
Jenny Sheridan
Anthony Simpson & Susan Boster
Brian Smith
Carl & Martha Tack
Katherine & Michael Yates

BOUNDARY-BREAKERS
John and Annoushka Ayton
Katie Bradford
Tim Fosberry
Edna & Peter Goldstein
Sue & Don Guiney
Rosanna Laurence
The David & Elaine Potter Charitable Foundation

MOVER-SHAKERS
Anonymous
Dianne & Michael Bienes*
Lois Cox
Cas & Philip Donald
Duncan Matthews QC
Ian & Carol Sellars
Jan & Michael Topham

HISTORY-MAKERS
Jack & Linda Keenan*
Miles Morland

MAJOR DONORS
Daniel & Joanna Friel
Deborah & Stephen Marquardt
Lady Sainsbury of Turville
NoraLee & Jon Sedmak*

*Supporters of the American Friends of the Royal Court

FOR THE ROYAL COURT

Royal Court Theatre, Sloane Square, London SW1W 8AS
Tel: 020 7565 5050 Fax: 020 7565 5001
info@royalcourttheatre.com, www.royalcourttheatre.com

Artistic Director **Dominic Cooke**
Associate Directors **Ramin Gray***, **Jeremy Herrin**,
Sacha Wares[+]
Artistic Associate **Emily McLaughlin**
Associate Producer **Diane Borger**
Diversity Associate **Ola Animashawun***
Education Associate **Lynne Gagliano***
Trainee Director (ITV Scheme) **Natalie Ibu**[‡]
PA to the Artistic Director **Victoria Reilly**

Literary Manager **Ruth Little**
Literary Associate **Terry Johnson***
Senior Reader **Nicola Wass**
Pearson Playwright **Daniel Jackson**[†]
Literary Assistant **Marcelo Dos Santos**

Associate Director International **Elyse Dodgson**
International Administrator **Chris James**
International Assistant **William Drew**

Studio Administrator **Clare McQuillan**
Writers' Tutor **Leo Butler***

Casting Director **Amy Ball**
Casting Assistant **Lotte Hines**

Head of Production **Paul Handley**
JTU Production Manager **Sue Bird, Tariq Rifaat**
Production Administrator **Sarah Davies**
Head of Lighting **Matt Drury**
Lighting Deputy **Nicki Brown**
Lighting Assistants **Stephen Andrews, Katie Pitt**
Lighting Board Operator **Tom Lightbody**
Head of Stage **Steven Stickler**
Stage Deputy **Duncan Russell**
Stage Chargehand **Lee Crimmen**
Chargehand Carpenter **Richard Martin**
Head of Sound **Ian Dickinson**
Sound Deputy **David McSeveney**
Sound Operator **Alex Caplen**
Head of Costume **Iona Kenrick**
Costume Deputy **Jackie Orton**
Wardrobe Assistant **Pam Anson**

ENGLISH STAGE COMPANY

President
Dame Joan Plowright CBE

Honorary Council
Sir Richard Eyre CBE
Alan Grieve CBE
Martin Paisner CBE

Council
Chairman **Anthony Burton**
Vice Chairman **Graham Devlin**

Executive Director **Kate Horton**
Head of Finance and Administration **Helen Perryer**
Planning Administrator **Davina Shah**
Senior Finance and Administration Officer **Martin Wheeler**
Finance Officer **Rachel Harrison***
Finance and Administration Assistant **Tessa Rivers**

Head of Communications **Kym Bartlett**
Marketing Manager **Becky Wootton**
Press & Public Affairs Officer **Stephen Pidcock**
Audience Development Officer **Gemma Frayne**
Communications Interns **Ruth Hawkins, Pippa Howie**
Sales Manager **Kevin West**
Deputy Sales Manager **Daniel Alicandro**
Box Office Sales Assistants **Ed Fortes, Shane Hough,
Ciara O'Toole**

Head of Development **Gaby Styles**
Senior Development Manager **Hannah Clifford**
Corporate Partnerships Manager **Sarah Drake** *
Development Officer **Lucy James**
Development Assistant **Penny Saward**

Theatre Manager **Bobbie Stokes**
Front of House Manager **Claire Simpson**
Deputy Theatre Manager **Daniel O'Neil**
Cafe Bar Managers **Paul Carstairs, Katy Mudge**
Bookshop Manager **Simon David**
Assistant Bookshop Manager **Edin Suljic***
Bookshop Assistant **Emily Lucienne** *
Building Maintenance Administrator **Jon Hunter**
Stage Door/Reception **Simon David***, **Paul Lovegrove,
Tyrone Lucas**

Thanks to all of our box office assistants, ushers and bar staff.

+ Sacha Wares' post is supported by the BBC through the
Gerald Chapman Fund.

** The post of Senior Reader is supported by NoraLee & Jon Sedmak through the
American Friends of the Royal Court Theatre.

‡ The post of Trainee Director is supported by ITV under the ITV Theatre
Director Scheme.

† This theatre has the support of the Pearson Playwrights' scheme, sponsored by
the Peggy Ramsay Foundation.

* Part-time.

Members
Jennette Arnold
Judy Daish
Sir David Green KCMG
Joyce Hytner OBE
Stephen Jeffreys
Wasfi Karni OBE
Phyllida Lloyd
James Midgley
Sophie Okonedo
Alan Rickman
Anita Scott
Katharine Viner
Stewart Wood

Polly Stenham
Tusk Tusk

ff

faber and faber

This edition first published in 2009
by Faber and Faber Limited
74–77 Great Russell Street, London WC1B 3DA

A CIP record for this book
is available from the British Library

Typeset by Country Setting, Kingsdown, Kent CT14 8ES
Printed in England by CPI Bookmarque, Croydon, Surrey

ISBN 978-0-571-24972-5

2 4 6 8 10 9 7 5 3

He hid the lobster.
You found it.

Smudge.
Pup.

This one's for you.

Acknowledgements

I would like to thank Jeremy Herrin, Dominic Cooke and Ruth Little for all their insight, support and belief.

My friends, Lisa, Nutty, Al, Toby, Matt, Johnny, and Harry. Thank you for listening to me rant and rave, for making all that tea and never letting me give up. And of course, Daisy. My sister. To whom this play is dedicated.

Characters

Eliot
fifteen

Maggie
fourteen

Finn
seven

Cassie

Katie
forties

Roland
forties

Man
from upstairs

Whenever possible this play should be performed
with actors of the same age, or very close to,
that of the young characters.

TUSK TUSK

Act One

SCENE ONE

Early morning. Present day. The open-plan living room of a flat in London. The front door leads directly into the room, as is the custom with town houses that have been divided into two living spaces. There is a kitchen area and a trapdoor that leads down into the basement. Closed floor-length curtains mask a large window leading out to the garden. A further door leads into adjoining bedrooms. The occupants have only just moved in. White moving boxes take the place of all furniture and furnishings with the exception of a large wooden table, a sofa and a dirty light fixture hanging from the ceiling. There is one mobile phone on the table.

The stage is dark. Maggie lets out a piercing scream. The lights go up.

We see Maggie, a girl of fourteen, standing petrified on the table. She is clutching a sheaf of money. As Eliot enters she stuffs it into her pocket.

Eliot charges in, rumpled from sleep. At fifteen he is still more of a boy then a young man, but only just.

Eliot What is it? What happened?

Maggie I saw –

Eliot What?

Maggie A mouse.

Eliot Is that it? Is that all?

Maggie Well, it could have been a rat.

Eliot I thought someone had broken in or –

Maggie I swear it looked at me.

Eliot Shut up.

Maggie Right at me with its beady little eyes. Ugh.

Eliot Don't be such a girl.

Maggie I am a girl.

Eliot Technically.

Maggie What do you mean, 'technically'? That I'm pretending? For a laugh?

Eliot No, just –

Maggie 'Cause let me tell you, it's not a laugh. Being a girl is a fucking mission.

Eliot I'm going back to bed.

Maggie There's a rat, Eliot.

Eliot I thought it was a mouse.

Maggie Does it matter? Do something.

Eliot Like what?

Maggie I don't know. Get rid of it. Please.

Eliot Maggie, I can't even see it.

Maggie You haven't looked.

Eliot I'm looking now.

Maggie Properly, Ellie.

Eliot Fine. I'll look 'properly'.

He pokes around the boxes half-heartedly. While his back is turned Maggie tries to stuff the money deeper into her pockets but some escapes and falls to the floor.

I can't see a thing. You probably imagined it . . . oh, hello . . . what's that?

Maggie tries to hide the money by stepping on it.

Maggie Nothing.

Eliot Show me.

Maggie Your flies are undone.

Eliot Show me.

Maggie You look like a flasher.

Eliot Give it, Maggie.

Maggie Like one of those weird people in the park –

He yanks it from under her foot and backs away, doing up his flies.

Ouch.

Eliot Fifty quid! Where did you find this?

Maggie . . .

Eliot Where, Maggie?

Maggie I um . . . it . . .

She looks suspicious, rams her hand further into her pocket.

Eliot What's in your pocket?

Maggie shrugs.

You've got more, haven't you?

Maggie No.

Eliot Show me your hands.

Maggie My hands are cold.

He yanks her hand out of her pocket. Money falls to the floor.

Eliot My God, what did you do, mug someone?

Maggie It's not that much.

He counts.

Eliot Two hundred quid! We're loaded.

Maggie Give it back.

Eliot Where did you find it?

Maggie In one of the boxes.

Eliot You genius . . . let's get takeaway.

Maggie It's eight in the morning.

Eliot So?

Maggie You can't get takeaway at eight in the morning.

Eliot We're in London. You can get anything at eight in the morning. Come on, let's have a Chinese breakfast . . .

Maggie Give it back, Ellie.

Eliot Dim sum yum.

Maggie I'm serious. I want to keep it.

Eliot No way. We're splitting it.

Maggie It's bill money, Eliot. It's not for crap. It's for emergencies.

Eliot Well, we don't have any bills to pay, do we? We only just got here.

Maggie Would you be sensible please. Just for a second. I'm better with money, you know I am, and we have to be careful –

Eliot Sensible? You're the one screaming over a pretend mouse.

Maggie IT WAS A RAT!

Eliot Oh I see. I understand now.

Maggie What?

Eliot No. It's OK. I've read about this. I know what to expect.

Maggie What are you talking about?

Eliot It's that time, isn't it?

Maggie Don't you dare –

Eliot It's OK. Really. I understand. Things get stressful. Hormones flapping all over the place. No. It's fine. You don't need to explain your mood. I understand. It's nature, after all.

Maggie Put the money on the table.

Eliot Maggie, look, you've dripped on the floor. A little splodge of blood –

Maggie Put it there right now.

Eliot It's like a Borrower's been murdered.

Maggie NOW, ELIOT!

Eliot I don't think that's wise, do you? I mean, you're probably not thinking straight. Also, you know what they say . . .

Maggie Shut up –

Eliot You can't trust something that bleeds for five days and doesn't die.

She pounces on him, he holds her hands up and she struggles, feline, but he is too strong.

Maggie I hate you I hate you I hate you.

There is a knocking on the door. They freeze. They glance at each other. Another knock. Their faces light up. Eliot slowly releases Maggie's hands. He puts his fingers to his lips. Eliot creeps to the door and peeks through the peephole. He shakes his head. Maggie's shoulders sag.

Maggie (*whispers*) Who then?

Eliot The guy from upstairs.

Maggie Again?

Eliot nods.

What does he want?

Eliot Shhh . . .

The knocking stops. The man appears to have left.

Maggie Maybe we should answer next time.
We can't avoid him for ever.

Eliot We don't have to avoid him for ever, do we?

Maggie We could make something up.

Eliot Like what?

Maggie I don't know, we could say –

Eliot No way. No other people involved. We agreed.

Maggie It might get him off our backs.

Eliot On our backs more like. Did you learn nothing from last time?

Maggie It's just he's going to see us coming in and out, it just seems more sensible –

Eliot It's simple, we'll go out at night. Like bats.

Maggie What if we went upstairs and introduced ourselves? We could forge a letter from –

Eliot No.

Maggie I just –

Eliot I said no.

Maggie Don't talk to me like that.

Eliot Will you shut up about this?

Maggie I'm not your wench.

Eliot If I let you keep the money, will you shut up?

Maggie All of it?

Eliot Most of it.

Maggie Ninety per cent of it?

Eliot Deal.

*He spits on his hand and holds it out to shake
Maggie's. She looks at him with disdain.*

What? That's what we always do.

Maggie Times have changed. Your spit has become
disgusting to me.

Eliot Ouch. Pain. Deep in my heart.

Maggie You have become disgusting to me.

Eliot Arrows tipped in wit. I'm injured. Help me.

Maggie Grow up.

Eliot What's the rush about?

He flops on the sofa.

Is there any food? I'm starving . . .

Maggie Sorry, Peter Pan, forgive me. Did I not prepare
you breakfast?

Eliot Evidently, wench, you did not.

She hits her own forehead.

What are you doing?

She does it again.

Stop it. You're being weird.

Maggie I'm punishing myself for being a terrible human being. Obviously making your breakfast is the first thing I should have done. Instead of waking up early, scratching around for cash, and watching my phone. What I should have been doing was rustling you up one of those little trays, with a single flower in a wine glass and teeny tiny pots of jam and a folded newspaper, ever so crisply tucked between the teeny tiny pots of jam –

Eliot I get your point, cut it out –

Maggie And in the tiny space between the newspaper and the teeny tiny pots of jam I should have probably sprinkled some rose petals because –

Eliot You know sarcasm is the lowest form of wit.

Maggie (*sarcastic*) Really? Is it?

Eliot Is there really no food . . .?

Maggie There's some tins and stuff. Stuff we brought down.

Eliot Chinese it is.

Maggie Do we really have to stay inside all day?

Eliot Think of it as a lie-in.

Maggie Where's Finn?

Eliot Snoozing.

Maggie Have you got your phone?

Eliot It's in the other room.

Maggie ELIOT!

Eliot What? I'll be able to hear it from here.

Maggie What if you don't? Eliot, Jesus. That was all you had to do.

Eliot Relax, would you.

Maggie We can't miss a call. We have to have them with us all the time. Come on. We've been through this.

Eliot OK, OK.

Maggie Go and get it.

Eliot Now?

Maggie Yes now.

> *He exits to get the phone. While he does so, Maggie carefully hides the money. He re-enters and puts his phone on the table next to Maggie's.*

Eliot Happy now?

Maggie Ecstatic.

> *He regards her.*

Eliot Has anyone ever told you . . .

Maggie What?

Eliot When you're angry –

Maggie I'm not angry –

Eliot Menstrual, whatever. You know who you look like? Just a little. But it is uncanny.

Maggie Enlighten me.

> *Small pause.*

Eliot Margaret Thatcher.

Maggie Shut up.

Eliot I'm serious. When your face catches the light. It's remarkable.

Maggie Leave me alone, Ellie.

Eliot I was trying to be nice.

Maggie Just go back to bed, all right? I'm not up for it this morning.

Eliot She was a very sexy lady. Besides. You were named after her.

Maggie I was not.

Eliot Were so. Mum told me.

Maggie She did not.

Eliot She did. Thatcher was a hero of hers.

Maggie starts to laugh.

What?

Maggie Can you not see the joke? Tell me you can . . . that's hysterical.

Eliot Why?

Maggie Think about it.

Eliot I don't get it.

Maggie Well, let's put it this way. I'd say her hero was a kind of cross between Marilyn Monroe and . . . Rosemary West . . . that would make more sense.

Eliot Maggie!

Maggie You know what I mean. Thatcher? She must have been joking.

Eliot She wasn't. You're the proof.

Maggie Yeah, and you were named after T. S. Eliot.

Eliot He is my namesake, yes.

Maggie Name a poem.

Eliot . . . ?

Maggie Just one.

Eliot Ummm . . . 'Romping in the Fields?'

Maggie Forget it. Feel my neck.

Eliot Not this again.

Maggie Feel it.

He does.

Eliot It's a gland, Maggie.

Maggie It's a lump. It's a proper lump.

Eliot I have one, see.

He puts her hand on his neck.

Maggie It's not the same.

Eliot You're not dying. This is exactly the same as that headache.

Maggie I had it for two weeks.

Eliot You wanted a brain scan.

Maggie Better safe than sorry.

Eliot You're not dying.

Maggie Promise?

Eliot Promise.

Beat.

Weirdo.

They are on the sofa now. She relaxes a little.

I'm hungry.

Maggie You know what I do have . . .

Eliot What?

Maggie I saved it from the journey down. A Twix.

Eliot Well crack it open.

Maggie It's a bit squashed.

They split it in two.

I'm sleepy.

She leans against him.

Eliot I heard you pattering last night. For ages.

Maggie I couldn't sleep.

Eliot Pitter-patter.

Maggie Bunnies patter. I don't patter. I pace. I was pacing.

Eliot Aw. Honey bunny.

Maggie Bloody bunny.

Eliot Bloody bunny funny.

Maggie Crummy bunny not sunny but bloody.

Eliot There she is.

Maggie (*really sleepy now*) Here I am.

She closes her eyes. Small pause.

Eliot . . .

Eliot Yeah?

Maggie I don't need to worry, do I?

Eliot About the lump? No, Maggie.

Maggie No . . . not that . . . you know . . . this.

Eliot Of course you don't.

Maggie It's only been a day.

Eliot Exactly.

Maggie It's fine.

Eliot It's completely fine. Get some sleep.

Maggie You'll watch the phones?

Eliot Shhh . . .

Maggie You have to watch them.

Eliot I'll watch them.

Maggie Don't let me sleep for long.

Eliot Let's swap night-time with daytime. I'll wake you when it's dark.

Maggie Like bats.

Eliot (*Irish accent*) Like wee bats.

She dozes off.
    Eliot slides his arm out from underneath her. He covers her with a blanket. He stands up and stretches. He pulls out a pack of cigarettes and puts one in his mouth but can't find a lighter. Hungry for his cigarette, he rifles through the room and stumbles upon the hidden money. Checking to see that Maggie isn't watching, he pockets two notes. Grinning, he lights his cigarette and saunters into the other room.

SCENE TWO

*That evening. It is dark outside. Maggie is still asleep on
the sofa. Finn charges into the room. A skinny boy of
seven, he is wearing only his underwear and a toy crown.
An old-fashioned toy gun pokes out of his waistband. He
has tribal stripes in lipstick on his cheekbones and chest.
His hands and feet are splattered with paint. He tries to
clean his hands by wiping them on the sofa. It doesn't
work. Maggie stirs. He spies a packet of Eliot's cigarettes
on the table. He picks one up and plays with it,
pretending to be smoking. He picks up the lighter and
considers it. There is a sound of the key in the door. Finn
darts behind the curtains.*

*Eliot enters holding a bag of Chinese takeaway. He has
the same tribal lipstick marks as Finn and a silk scarf tied
around his head. He removes his coat and we see he has
marks on his chest also.*

*Eliot creeps cheekily up to Maggie and gets up close to
her ear. He makes a loud Red Indian call directly in her
ear. She jumps awake.*

Maggie Twat.

Eliot Breakfast . . .

Maggie Are you serious?

Eliot Oh yeah.

Maggie What time is it?

Eliot Nine-ish. You slept all day.

Maggie Are you wearing lipstick?

Eliot Warpaint, babes.

Maggie Lipstick, idiot.

Eliot I'm a modern man . . . I'm a metrosexual warrior . . . an urban fox if you will –

Maggie Did you go out like that?

Eliot Yeah, I did. And let me tell you, it's a hit with the ladies –

She pokes at the Chinese.

Maggie Eliot, it's cold.

Eliot I took a while.

Maggie It's down the road.

Eliot I met someone . . . I made a lady friend.

Maggie In that get-up? You're joking.

Eliot Told you, ladies love it. Shows I'm not self-conscious. Which is, by the way, apparently, very sexy –

Maggie Spare me the details, Rambo. How are we going to heat this up?

Eliot In the microwave.

Maggie Look around?

He does.

Do you see a microwave?

Eliot Whoops.

Maggie You didn't get anything else, did you?

Eliot I got some prawn crackers and um . . . well –

Maggie I give up. Where's Finn?

Eliot Hiding . . .

A small giggle is heard from behind the curtain.

Oh where could he be I wonder?

Eliot puts his hand to his mouth and makes another Red Indian call.

Maggie Oh my God.

He does it again.

I'm in a bad Enid Blyton novel.

Eliot Shhh . . .

Suddenly Finn bursts through the curtains. He aims his gun at Eliot.

Finn BE STILL!

Eliot Have mercy on me, Max, have mercy –

He shoots at Eliot. A red flag pops out of the end of the gun. Eliot drops to the floor, 'dead'. Finn blows the top of his gun with a flourish. Then he spies Maggie and reloads.

Finn I said 'Be still . . .'

Maggie I've heard about you.

Finn takes aim.

You're Max, you're famous.

Finn I am a famous outlaw, yes.

Maggie I can't believe it's you. King of All Wild Things.

She bows.

Finn It is I. Yes.

Maggie Just one question, if you please.

Finn Only one, because then I must shoot you.

Maggie At what point did you get the gun, because in the famous story –

Finn Legend.

Maggie Forgive me. In the famous legend, young Max had no gun. He just tamed them with his eyes. He also wore a wolf suit. Are you really Max?

Finn How dare you!

Maggie But where is your wolf suit?

Eliot He traded it for the gun.

Finn Now say your prayers, ladeee.

Maggie Our father who art in heaven hallowed be thy name thy kingdom come thy will be done on earth as it is in heaven . . .

Finn aims at her, but just as he's about to shoot he spies the mouse.

Finn I saw it! I saw the mouse!

Maggie Where?

Finn There!

Eliot What? 'There on the stair'?

Maggie ELIOT, do something.

Eliot 'A little mouse with clogs on'?

Finn It went into the hole.

Maggie Block the hole. Trap it.

Eliot does so.

Is it safe?

Finn Why are you scared? It's only a mouse.

Maggie It's a rat, Finn, and rats are evil. When bad people die they come back as rats.

Finn Like Hitler?

Maggie Just like Hitler. In fact that rat is probably Hitler.

Eliot Don't tell him that.

Maggie Why not?

Eliot Because it's not true. Finn, it's just an animal. Maggie doesn't like it because she's a girl and she's scared of everything –

Maggie Finn, that rat murdered twelve million people. It deserves to die.

Finn So we live with Hitler.

Maggie Sort of.

Finn Cool.

Eliot Stop it, Maggie, you'll give him weird ideas.

Maggie I happen to believe in reincarnation.

Eliot So you're a Buddhist now?

Maggie You bought him a gun. Someone's got to redress the balance.

Eliot I was modernising the story.

Maggie I'm sure Sendak will be delighted. What next? *Max the Terrorist*? *Where the Crack Dealers Are*?

Eliot I had to entertain him somehow. You've been asleep all day.

Maggie Well, it looks like you've had a riot. Any calls?

Eliot No. You hungry, Finn?

Maggie Are you sure?

Eliot I'm sure. Look, Finn. Grub.

Finn You were gone for ages.

Eliot Sorry, baby, it took a little while.

Finn Ages.

Eliot Look, Chinese yum.

Maggie is up and pacing. She is trying her phone again.

Maggie It's off.

Finn Ugh. It's cold –

Maggie Why is it still off?

Eliot So she's out of battery. Chill.

Finn I don't want it. I don't want it cold.

Eliot Finn, it's summer Chinese. Summer Chinese is always cold.

Maggie Did she take her charger?

Eliot Just have a little bit.

Maggie Eliot!

Eliot What?

Maggie Did she take her charger?

Eliot I don't know. Probably.

Maggie Did you see her slip it in her bag or something?

Eliot I don't know, you stayed with her longer – if anyone saw her pack it, it was you. Please, Finn. Eat something.

Maggie I told you. I left just after you. I went for a walk.

Eliot Then we don't know, do we? Just one bite, Finn.

Maggie We should look. Help me look.

Eliot Just one mouthful, Finn. It's good. I promise.

Finn No.

Maggie What box could it be in?

Eliot Open wide.

Maggie ELIOT!

Eliot I don't know.

Maggie Think.

Eliot Her stuff's in the bedroom. Maybe in there.

Maggie Some help?

Eliot I'm a little busy here.

She storms out.
He takes a theatrical bite.

See, Finn, it's very refreshing cold.

Finn I want cereal.

Eliot In China, this it what karate fighters have for breakfast. Rice is like . . . Coco Pops for ninjas.

Finn Really . . .

Eliot Oh yeah . . .

Maggie (*offstage*) Fiiiiiiiiinnnnnnnn!

Finn Oh no.

Maggie (*offstage*) Fiiiinnnnnnnn, get in here!

Eliot What have you done?

Finn runs and hides behind one of the boxes.
Maggie storms back in.

Maggie Where is he?

Eliot What's happened?

Maggie Finn, come out right now.

Eliot Come on, it can't be –

Maggie RIGHT NOW!

Eliot There's no need to shout.

Maggie Go check it out. Check out Mum's room.

Eliot I'm sure it's not so bad. We just need to remain calm.

Maggie Go look.

He does. Finn peeks out from behind a box. Maggie gestures for him to come out.

Eliot (*offstage*) Fiiiiiiiiinnnnnnnnn!

Finn hides behind the box again.
Eliot storms back in.

You little . . . get out from behind there. NOW!

Maggie So calm.

Eliot NOW!

He yanks him out by his elasticised waist and plonks him on the table.

Why is Mummy's room covered in paint?

Finn I . . .

He turns to Maggie.

Eliot What are we going to do? It's everywhere. The carpet. The walls. It's all over her clothes.

Maggie At least it's her favourite colour.

Finn giggles a little.

Eliot This is not funny. *Why* are you finding this funny? We've ruined her stuff. Her dresses. She loves her dresses. We've ruined them. Ruined them –

Maggie laughs again.

Maggie Sorry. I just can't take you seriously dressed like that.

Eliot IT'S NOT FUNNY!

He rips his headband off and paces the room.

What are we going to do? . . . Oh God . . . We'll never get it out of the carpet. Let alone the walls. And her stuff. Oh no . . .

Maggie What happened, Finn? Did you knock the pot over?

Finn I wanted it to be a surprise.

Eliot Well, congratulations, Finn. It was.

Finn You were gone for ages and Maggie was asleep and I got bored. And I remembered she wanted her room painted blue. Like at home. And that's why we bought the paint at the shop. And I saw the paint on the floor. And it was so blue. I thought I could start.

Maggie Start what?

Finn The painting.

Maggie I told you not to leave him alone.

Eliot I didn't, did I? You were here.

Maggie I was asleep. Not the same thing.

Eliot We were starving. I had to go and get food.

Maggie But that's not all you did, was it? You said yourself you were gone for ages. Chatting up girls.

Eliot It wasn't that long.

Maggie It was long enough. Idiot.

Finn Can I get down now?

Eliot/Maggie NO!

Eliot Look. It's fine. We'll use some of that money to dry clean the clothes. We'll make the best of the rest.

Maggie We don't have enough to do that, Eliot.

Eliot Yes we do.

Maggie What the hell do you know about dry cleaning, Rambo? It costs a fortune.

Eliot We've got loads of money.

Maggie We have to be careful with it.

Eliot This is important, Maggie.

Maggie Not as important as eating.

Eliot We can eat pasta, can't we? We only need a bit of cash.

Maggie How many times. You don't know that.

Eliot Yes I do.

Maggie You don't. You just don't.

Eliot We can't just leave her clothes there to rot.

Maggie Why not? That's what's she's . . . We can't risk it, Eliot.

Eliot We have to. Come on. You don't want to see the look on her face when she walks into that room. You just don't.

Maggie Why do you care so much?

Eliot Why don't you?

Maggie Because they're clothes, Eliot. Stupid clothes. She doesn't wear them half the time anyway –

Eliot She does so. She does go out. She wore one last week –

Maggie They're of *no* use to us. And we have to think about us.

   Beat.

Someone has to.

Eliot I am thinking about us. I am.

Maggie Then think, idiot. What are we going to eat if we've spent this money . . . What? A vintage dress? A hat? Come on . . . it's not like before, it's not like back at home. We don't know anyone. We can't go and beg a tin of baked beans off a friend's mum. We can't put stuff on credit at the shop. It's a big city and we're little. We have to be careful.

Eliot Half and half. Just dry clean her favourite two things. Come on.

Maggie Look . . . we made a deal, Ellie. If you want me to sit tight and not call anyone, I'll do that. But only if I'm in charge of the cash. I'll only do it this way. I'll be as hippy-dippy and positive as you want, but we have to have money. Just in case.

   Pause.

Eliot You drive a hard bargain.

Maggie So do you.

Eliot Fine. But she'll never let you forget about it. You know that. She'll be livid.

Maggie I look forward to it.

Eliot You're digging your own grave.

Maggie Don't say that.

Eliot Why? Are you getting all lumpy and paranoid?

Maggie No. It's not that. Just don't say stuff like that.

Eliot Fine.
  Digging your own . . . sex dungeon, then? How about that?

Maggie You're not funny.

Eliot Yes I am.

Maggie You're really not.

Eliot You're just immune to my charms 'cause you're my sister.

Maggie Don't be weird.

Eliot You're the weird one. Lumpy McLump.

Finn Am I still in trouble?

Maggie/Eliot YES!

SCENE THREE

Early morning. The den is built. A small lamp has been put inside making the space glow. Finn's crown sits on the table top. Music is playing.
  Maggie is searching the boxes furiously. Eliot enters. He stands and watches her for a moment. She doesn't notice.

Eliot What are you doing?

Maggie You scared me. I thought you were asleep.

35

She goes back to searching.
  There is a knocking at the door. Eliot quickly turns the music down. Maggie goes to the peephole.

It's him again.

Eliot Shhh . . .

Maggie Let's have some fun.

Eliot No, Maggie. Don't.

Maggie grins at him, taunting.
  Eliot shakes his head. Furious, he creeps up to grab her but just before he does she swiftly puts the door on the latch and opens it a little.

Man This can't go on. I need my sleep. You're banging and screaming. That infernal radio. It's just not right. I have a good mind to report you –

Maggie No. Don't do that.

Man Your parents. I want to speak to them. Where's the little boy? I've seen the little boy. He relieved himself in my bushes.

Maggie snorts with laughter.

In broad daylight.

Maggie turns to Eliot and grins: she now adopts an eastern European accent.

Maggie I am so sorry. The boy. He is not – how can I say this? Trained.

Man Pardon?

Maggie You know, trained. Like a dog. He is a little backward. We do our best, you see. We replace your flowers, no problem.

Man Why are you talking like that? Would you open the door?

Maggie Like what?

Man Like a Polack. Open the damn door.

Maggie I am from Warsaw. I am nanny. In my country we do not open the door to strangers.

Man Nanny?

Maggie I am nanny for wee child.

Man You're too young.

Maggie In my country we all look young. It's a good thing, no?

Man But before you spoke English.

Maggie My English sometimes good, sometimes bad.

Man Then where is your employer? I need to speak to your employer.

Eliot sinks to the floor.

Maggie You talk to my boyfriend. He is an English fellow. You like him. I smell it.

Man Let me in.

Maggie CLAUDE!

She shouts in Eliot's ear.

Claude! An Englishman, a gentleman for you.

She drags Eliot to a gap in the door.

I was telling the nice man about you. About our job.

Man I need to speak to your employers. You have been disturbing me.

Eliot I'm really very sorry about that. You know kids. Poor boy. Misses his mother, we've just been trying to entertain him. Keep his spirits up. You know.

Man He took a pee in my bushes.

Maggie Isn't he handsome?

Man Pardon?

Maggie My boyfriend. Isn't he handsome?

Eliot Ignore her. Her English is terrible.

Man I want to speak to your employers. This is ridiculous.

Eliot I'll ensure our employer is informed when she returns.

Man When will that be?

Eliot She's on a business trip, so not for at least a week.

Man How old are you?

Maggie He is my toyboy. My boytoy.

Eliot I'll let my employer know that you called. In the meantime, we'll reduce the noise.

Man I want to call her. Your employer. You must have a number for her. For emergencies.

Eliot I wouldn't want to alarm her.

Man I think she should be alarmed.

Eliot Look. I promise we'll keep the noise down. I'll get our employer to contact you as soon as she gets back. I assure you, no more trouble. We'll keep a better eye on the boy.

Man Hmm.

Eliot We're so sorry.

Man I'll be expecting her.

The Man leaves. Maggie starts to laugh.

Eliot Shhh . . .

Maggie Priceless.

Eliot You idiot. He knows something's up.

Maggie Why are you worried? We got away with it.

Eliot You're such a tit.

Maggie (*accent*) Claude, never insult my tits.

He laughs.

Eliot Idiot.

She starts searching the boxes again.

Maggie How can we have so much but so little? It's ridiculous. I knew we should have labelled the boxes. I knew it.

She finds the charger.

Brilliant.

She holds it up to him.

That's just brilliant, Eliot.

She throws it to the floor.

Eliot Maggie come on . . . noise.

Maggie You know what that means, don't you?

Eliot It means nothing. She barely knew how to charge her phone anyways –

Maggie You know what it means.

Eliot Shhh . . .

Maggie It means she didn't plan to go.

Eliot She never plans to go, she just . . . It's her way –

Maggie 'Her way' – if I hear that one more time I'm going to –

Eliot Shhh . . .

Maggie (*quietly*) – scream.

Eliot It's just a piece of plastic, there's no need to –

Maggie It means she just left, it means she didn't –

Eliot It doesn't mean anything.

Maggie I'm scared, Eliot.

Eliot sits down.

I know she's done this before and I know it's always been all right but . . .

Eliot But what?

Pause.

Maggie I just have this feeling.

Eliot Do you not think that might have something to do with the . . .

He points between his legs.

Maggie Jesus, Ellie, I'm serious.

Eliot Sorry. I know.

Maggie I just think we should tell someone. A grown-up.

Small pause.

Eliot We made a deal, Maggie –

Maggie But I didn't know she left this, did I? This changes things.

Eliot It changes nothing, Mags. Come on. Stick to the plan.

Maggie What about her old boyfriend, that posh guy – ?

Eliot Posho Rollo? And give him the satisfaction? After what he did to her? No way.

Maggie What about Katie then?

Eliot His wife. Don't be stupid.

Maggie She sent us something.

Maggie hands him an envelope.

Eliot When?

Maggie shrugs.

Maggie It was under all those flyers. There was no stamp.

Eliot reads from the card.

Eliot 'On a sunny day you could take the kids down to the river, there's a perfectly sweet little café . . .' Bla bla bla.

Maggie I think it's nice.

Eliot I think it's creepy. She shouldn't be nice to us when it's completely obvious.

Maggie She's just being polite.

Eliot Ugh. It's so English. I can't stand it.

Maggie She said if we needed anything? I don't see the harm in just asking if she's seen her –

Eliot No, Maggie. No way. It'll get straight back to him. No way.

Maggie There must be someone else then? Another boyfriend, one of the ones from before.

Eliot What other ones?

Maggie The string of useless fucks she used to fuck.

Eliot Maggie, shhh . . .

Maggie (*harsh whisper*) Oh, don't get precious on me, you know what I'm talking about.

Eliot I do not.

Maggie You have a really selective memory, don't you?

Eliot Just don't talk like that, I don't like it.

Maggie I'm being honest.

Eliot You're being harsh.

Maggie She had lots of sex, Eliot, get over it.

Eliot Please, have some respect.

Maggie She ate men like air.

Eliot Drop it. Drop it right now. I don't like it.

Maggie Fine. Keep sleepwalking, Bambi. Keep sleep-walking.

   Beat.

There must be someone, though. Someone we can tell.

Eliot Who? Who wouldn't tell on us? It would be different if it was just us two, but with Finn . . . you know what will happen. No. Sorry. We've got to keep our mouths shut. It's the only option.

Maggie (*slams the table*) Fuck.

Eliot But look on the bright side, Mags, we can do whatever the hell we want in the meantime. It's quite nice to have the place to ourselves. None of that headache stuff. The endless tiptoeing. Having to leave the lights off. We should look on it as a holiday . . .

Maggie I like the lights off.

Eliot We could get a strobe.

Maggie (*getting upset now*) Eliot, this is horrible, you can't pretend it isn't . . .

I miss my friends. Everyone's summer is going on without us . . . They're going camping, sneaking into the pub. It's not fair. I hate it here. I wish we'd never moved.

Eliot We could go back up and visit.

Maggie We can't afford it, it's like seventy quid each. Might as well be Timbuktu for how far away it feels. Stupid trains. Ugh, look at this place. It's horrible. It's gloomy, it's –

Eliot So it needs some work.

Maggie Ellie, your 'room' is the basement. Have you even been down there? It's full of dust and there isn't a light and . . .

Eliot There's a window.

Maggie Hardly.

Maggie Whatever, it gives me the shivers . . . the whole place does.

Eliot You're overreacting, we'll fix it up.

Maggie Finn agrees with me, you heard him screaming, he won't sleep anywhere without us. He thinks it's haunted.

Eliot He's a kid.

Maggie So am I.

Beat.

So are you.

Eliot I'm not really a kid, I'll be sixteen in, what . . . eight days . . . How many hours is that?

43

Maggie One hundred and ninety-two.

Eliot Wow.

Maggie I don't feel wow.

Beat.

I'm really worried, Ellie . . .
There's an armada in my head.

Eliot Hey . . .

Maggie Things on fire.

Eliot Come on, Maggie. It really isn't that bad –

Maggie We need a plan.

Eliot We've got a plan. One, at least one of us is always here. Two, don't let anyone know. Three, check the phones every half-hour, it's all we can –

Maggie We need a deadline.

Eliot Don't talk like that.

Maggie At least for my mind.

Pause.

Eliot OK. I don't think this is necessary, but if you're going to get all melodramatic about it –

She throws something at him.

Ow . . .

Maggie I'm serious, Eliot.

Eliot Fine. Let's make it my birthday. That's ages away.

Maggie Then what will we do?

Eliot It won't get to that, Maggie.

Maggie I know, but –

Eliot It won't. OK? It just won't.

Maggie You promise?

Eliot I swear.

Maggie What makes you so sure?

Eliot (*mocking her*) 'I just have this feeling.'

Maggie Really, though?

Eliot Have faith, little one. Have faith.

Maggie Even if you . . .

Eliot Even what?

Maggie Even if . . .

His phone beeps, he checks it.

Eliot Right, I've got to pop out. What were you saying?

Maggie What do you mean you've got to go? Go where?

Eliot I was just going to dash out to –

Maggie Where? It's six-thirty in the morning.

Pause.

You're going to see that girl, aren't you? That's where you were going when you thought I was in bed – (*Louder.*) You were going to sneak out . . .

Eliot I was going to leave you a note. It's just I said I'd meet her for coffee.

Maggie Coffee? At dawn?

Eliot She went out clubbing. I wanted to see her again. I promised.

Maggie That's not fair, Ellie, I'm not your nanny, you can't just hop off as soon as he's down for the night . . . day . . . whatever . . . and leave me holding the fort. You can't just do that.

45

Eliot I'd do it for you.

Maggie Like hell you would.

Eliot Please, Mags, I really like her. I'm just going for breakfast.

Maggie Oh, breakfast now is it?

Eliot I knew you would react like this.

Maggie Like what?

Eliot Like this.

Maggie Fine. Go.

Eliot It's just for an hour.

Maggie Bring back some milk, Romeo.

Eliot Stop it – can't you be happy for me?

Maggie Happy for you? It's not like you're pregnant, it's not like you're getting promoted. Happy for you? Get a grip.

Eliot I'm making a friend.

Maggie Your trying to get laid, slight difference.

Eliot Hey, gotta make the most of it while I'm still illegal. Only eight days to go. If it happens now it will be classed as rape . . . Brilliant.

Maggie doesn't smile.

Come on, give me a smile or something. Just one. Smile for rape. Give me a big grin for rape.

She grins manically.

There we go. There's my girl. Dark as ditchwater. Just how I like her.

Maggie Couldn't you go later, when Finn's awake?

Eliot She's waiting for me now.

Beat.

It's an hour, Mags, come on . . .

Maggie shrugs agreement.

I love you.

Maggie Ugh!

She puts her middle finger up at him.

Eliot Just tuck yourself up with Finn. I'll be back before you know it.

He is nearly out of the door.

Maggie Eliot . . .

Eliot What?

She can't tell him.

Maggie Remember the milk.

He blows her a kiss as he exits.
Maggie gets a piece of material hidden underneath one of the sofa cushions – a piece of her mother's clothing. She buries her face in it, inhaling the smell. She lies on the sofa. She twists the material gently in her hands, like an infant. She closes her eyes.

SCENE FOUR

Three hours later. The stage is dark. There is only the faint glow of daylight from behind the curtains. The set is the same as before.
Maggie is sleeping on the sofa. She wakes up with a jolt. We see her at her most childlike now. Rumpled and confused, moving slowly. She checks the time.

47

Maggie (*softly*) Ellie, is that you?

She looks around the room. She seems about to climb off the table, but the boxes take on looming shapes. Frightened, she stays where she is.

If this is some kind of game then I'm not playing. 'Cause it's not funny. Not here. So stop being a twat and come out. Please come out.

Her breathing gets more jagged. She grabs her phone; she calls Eliot; no reply.

Finn, baby, Finn, wake up.

She turns on the little lamp underneath the table.

Finn?

He stirs but stays half asleep.
She lifts the sleepy child into her arms. She stands, clinging to him. She rocks him in the pretence of soothing him but is really soothing herself. The light and the warmth of his body begin to calm her.

Finn What are you doing?

Maggie You had a bad dream.

Finn I don't remember.

Maggie You did. You were calling 'Maggie, Maggie'.

Finn I think I dreamt of boats.

Maggie See, you can remember.

Finn It wasn't bad. I had my own boat. Just for me.

Maggie Tell me about it.

Finn It was green, made out of golden-syrup cans.

Maggie You love golden syrup.

Finn I do.

He appears to go back to sleep.

Maggie Do you want some now? We have one can left.

Finn Now?

Maggie As a treat. We won't tell anyone.

Finn I'm not hungry.

Maggie But you've been sailing all day.

Finn That's true.

Maggie I could heat it up . . . somehow.

Finn Mmm . . .

She smells his hair.

Maggie But you have to stay awake.

Finn Is it late?

Maggie It's very late.

Finn Cool . . .

She smiles and smells his hair. He falls asleep again. She carries him to the sofa. She tries to wake him up again. He bats her away. She curls up with him, pulling a blanket over them. A few moments pass. She cannot sleep.

Giggling and scrabbling at the lock can be heard. The door opens, revealing Eliot and Cassie. Eliot's hair is styled differently. They have swapped coats. Eliot looks ridiculous in Cassie's pink jacket and she looks swamped in his.

Maggie becomes alert but remains still. With the blanket covering them, Eliot can't see her but the audience know that she is awake and listening.

Cassie Wow . . .
Nice house. Why so dark?

Eliot Shhh . . . we're nocturnal.

He checks the den: satisfied that his siblings are in the other room, he becomes more confident.

Cassie What's in these boxes?

Eliot Little Miss Curious. Come here.

She comes to him. He stares at her, he smiles.

Cassie Don't, you'll make me laugh, you look like –

Eliot Who?

Cassie (*giggles*) My nan. It's her coat.

Eliot Kinky.

He puckers his lips.

Cassie Don't! You're freaking me –

Eliot Don't you like old ladies? . . . I like old ladies.

Cassie She's dead.

Eliot Right. God. Sorry. I'll take it off.

Cassie I'm joking. Keep it on. You look funny.

Eliot Funny?

Cassie Cute.

Eliot Shut up.

Cassie Shut me up, then.

They kiss gently, then harder. Hands begin to wander. Coats slip off. They both pull away a little breathless.

Greedy.

Eliot Hungry.

He searches through some cupboards. There is nothing. Only jam.

Fuck all. What we do have, in spades, is um, well, jam. No bread. But some lovely gooey Prince's Trust, ethnically-cleansed and completely-free-from-even-a-tang-of-guilt jam. Or preserve, if you'd prefer.

He regards the pot.

Stupid woman. Why leave jam? Why even pack jam? None of us even like it. It looks like cartoon blood. Ugh.

Cassie No thanks. I'm fine really.

Eliot But we don't want your belly all fizzing and tizzing with cider now, do we? There's that or . . . nothing really.

Cassie I'm fine.

She opens a can of cider.
  As he looks in the cupboards she comes up behind him and places the crown on his head. She turns him around.

Your Majesty.

Eliot Shouldn't you curtsy?

Cassie If the monarch does insist.

Eliot He does.

She hands him the cider. She curtsies, kneeling on the floor. She looks up at him.

Cassie Like this, My Lord?

Eliot Just like that.

She runs her hands up his legs; she starts to undo his flies; Eliot moans softly.

At this point Maggie springs up.
Both Cassie and Eliot spring away from each other.

Jesus Christ!

He is trying to do up his flies.

You shouldn't jump out on people like that. You scared me.

Maggie (*dangerously even*) I scared you?

Eliot Cassie, this is my –

Maggie You don't know the meaning of scared.

Cassie Hi –

Ignoring her.

Maggie Scared is waking up and finding your –

Eliot I thought you'd still be asleep when I got back.

Maggie You said you'd be an hour. I waited up for you. Then I promised myself if I fell asleep that you'd be back when I woke up. Then I woke up and you weren't here. No one was here. Something went bump in my mind, went bump in the dark, and you weren't here . . .

Cassie I should –

Maggie No. You stay. He's used our dinner money to pay already, presumably.

Cassie is gobsmacked.

Eliot Take that back.

Maggie Sorry, was that rude, was that impolite . . . was that inconsiderate of me?

Eliot Take that back.

Maggie Fuck you, Your Majesty. (*She bows.*)

Cassie You have some nerve.

Eliot What?

Cassie Some nerve.

Eliot begins to laugh.

You find that funny, do you? Look at the state of your girlfriend. You twat –

Eliot She's my sister. My fourteen-year-old sister.

Cassie I thought –

Maggie Are you crazy? (*She lowers her voice.*) You were gone for hours. You don't even call to tell me you were going to be late –

Eliot I lost track of time –

Maggie You leave me. Alone. In this creepy house. Then you bring home some girl and start getting lewd with her in the same room as me and your seven-year-old brother. You're sick in the head.

Cassie has edged towards the door. She begins to open it.

Eliot No, don't go. Stay. Please.

Cassie I think –

Eliot Please. Just give us a minute. There's a garden. Here, have a fag. Go look around. She'll calm down –

Maggie Oh, will I?

Cassie I don't know –

Eliot Please.

She exits to another room.

Listen, Maggie, I thought –

Maggie You didn't think. You never think. I had to lie to Finn. Say you were out at the shops. He kept asking and asking. It was horrible. And just for a second, for a millisecond, I thought you had left, like . . . like it was all part of some magic trick. Black, masochistic magic.

Beat.

Only for a second though.

Eliot Millisecond.

Maggie It was a whole second.

Beat.

You look ridiculous in that crown.

Eliot hands her the cider. She considers, then takes it.

Did she call?

Eliot She will.

Maggie I can't stand this waiting. Staring at that little screen, begging it to ring. When the power-save comes on it's like the phone's winking. Its like it's in on it.

Eliot I'll watch them –

Maggie That won't help. It's messing with me, Eliot. It's grinding the corners of my mind. And when I woke up. I . . .

Eliot What?

Maggie I felt someone breathing on me. I thought it was you. Just here on my neck. I felt breath.

Eliot It was the wind. That's all.

Maggie slumps back down on the sofa.

Maggie Your hair looks different.

Eliot She styled it. Looks good, no?

She regards him.

Maggie You look different.

Beat.

Some fresh start this is . . . fuck.

Beat.

Eliot Do me a favour, Mags.

Maggie is examining the bag of cider.

Maggie Did you only get booze?

Eliot Tell her you're sorry about the hooker thing. Girls really don't like that stuff. It makes them shy.

Maggie What? By post to her pimp?

Eliot Stop it. I really like her.

Maggie Fine. I'll send her a fricking dove. Give me my own cider.

He opens one for her. She glugs it.

I bet you ate. I bet you took her to Nobu.

Eliot Easy on that.

Maggie Oh, now you're my big brother.

She glugs harder.

Eliot Seriously.

She glugs more. It runs down her chin.

Give it back.

Maggie Relax, we're on holiday, remember? She can bartend.

Beat.

Your new hairstyle's stupid. You look like a monkey.

Eliot Piss off.

Maggie You did a bit before, but now, wow . . .

Eliot Shhh . . . you'll wake Finn.

Maggie Aw, the animal protects his young.

Eliot I don't want to wake him.

Maggie With your monkey-squeals of passion? How thoughtful.

Eliot Take him to bed. Please.

Maggie I've been to bed, darling. I'm wide awake now. I want to play.

Eliot sighs.

I want to play with my monkey brother.

Eliot Enough –

Maggie I want to pick him for fleas. He brings back vermin. Dirty boy.

Eliot Stop it.

Maggie mocks monkey behaviour, jumping up and down on the sofa. She ends up with her arms locked around his neck.
Cassie enters cautiously.

Cassie I like your house. The blue room's pretty cool. Did someone spill –

Maggie Eliot did it. He's a bit of an artist. Well, he thinks he –

Eliot Shut up, Maggie –

Maggie busies herself picking Eliot for fleas.

Cassie What are you –?

Maggie Picking him for fleas. He gets them sometimes.

Eliot Get off.

He tries to shake her off but she clings on.

Maggie It takes a while. Little buggers love him. Suck his blood. That's why he's so pale.

Cassie Gross.

Maggie Don't be embarrassed, Ellie. She's probably caught them off you by now. They're pretty contagious.

Beat.

In fact . . . I think I can see some swarming above your head.

Eliot has had enough. He shoves Maggie off him.

Eliot She's fucking with you.

Maggie How rude. It was you who was about to do the fucking.

Eliot MAGGIE!

Maggie You oily little love-monkey. King of the love-monkeys.

Eliot She's like this sometimes. She gets . . . hyper.

Maggie Do I? I hadn't noticed. It's probably because all I've had to eat for twenty-four hours was cold takeaway, because you – You. Ran off to Nobu with all our money.

Eliot We didn't go to Nobu – what's all this stuff about Nobu?

Maggie I hear it's a very nice restaurant. Perfect for love-monkeys and their oily dates.

Eliot Enough. Take Finn to bed.

Maggie FINN!

Eliot Stop shouting.

Maggie ELIOT'S home.

Eliot Would you just –

Maggie He wants to play.

Eliot (*to Cassie*) I'm sorry.

Maggie He wants to play with his new friend and he wants us to go to bed. That's not fair, is it?

Finn (*baffled*) Who the bloody are you?

Cassie Wow. You guys just keep popping up.

Finn Who is she?

Cassie My name's Cassie, I'm a friend of your brother.

Eliot Maggie's going to take you to bed.

Maggie Am I?

Eliot So you can get a nice quiet sleep.

Maggie He wants us to go to bed so he can play with her.

Eliot That's not true.

Maggie It is though, isn't it?

Finn I want to play. I've been to sleep. For ages and ages.

Maggie Finn sailed the world.

Cassie Really?

Maggie And look where he's ended up? In a monkey jungle.

> *She mocks monkey behaviour again.*
>   *Finn laughs.*
>   *She heightens her performance, jumping above Finn on the sofa. He jumps with her.*

Eliot Christ.

Maggie 'Cause monkeys have the best time, don't they? They get to go wherever they want.

Maggie and Finn scamper among the boxes.

They get to climb all over the place. They get to climb all over each other.

She lifts Finn onto a stack of boxes.

They get to swing from the –

She reaches up to the light.

– trees.

She touches the glass.

Eliot Don't –

Finn tries to touch the light. His balance begins to go.

Maggie From the jewelled trees.

Finn stretches out to touch the light. The stack of boxes collapses from under him. He falls to the ground. A box falls on top of him. There is the sound of breaking china and glass. Finn lies motionless on the floor. Shattered china spills out around him.
    Eliot springs up and kneels next to Finn.

Eliot You idiot. You fucking idiot!

Maggie stands a little way away, mortified.

Help me! Christ, he's bleeding. He's bleeding. His head is bleeding. HELP ME!

He pulls Finn upwards into his arms. They are now sitting on the floor, with Finn awake, yet dazed and limp between Eliot's legs. Blood runs down his face from a cut above his eye. It is bright, bright red. Stunning.

Get something, anything. NOW!

Maggie pulls off her T-shirt and hands it to Eliot. He holds it against Finn's face, trying to staunch the blood. It is at this moment that the shock wears off and Finn begins to scream. The sound curdles the atmosphere of the room.

It's OK. You're OK. TELL HIM HE'S OK!

Finn screams again.

Help me. Maggie. Help me carry him.

Louder screams. More of the pain is dawning on Finn. Loud banging from above.
Together they carry him to the table. He screams. They lay him down. He wriggles like a kitten caught in barbed wire.

Hold his feet. HOLD HIS FEET!

Both girls hold his feet down.

Keep still, keep still. Finny, please. Stop wriggling. I need to see. Shhh. Please. Shhh . . . Please . . . shhh. Please . . . Brave boy. Isn't he? Brave boy. Shhh . . .

More screams, followed by banging from the flat above and sounds of the Man telling them to shut up. Eliot puts his hand over Finn's mouth.

You have to be quiet Finny. Shhh . . . You have to be quiet. Shhh . . .

Beat.

Ah . . . he bit me.

Cassie That's a good sign, it could mean he's not concussed –

Maggie But people can get concussed, can't they, later / when they fall asleep.

Eliot Shut up, Maggie. He's fine. Aren't you? He's fine. Shhh . . .

Cassie Keep his head up. If it's his nose / you must keep his head up.

Eliot It's not his nose. I don't think. There's too much blood. I can't see for the blood. Keep still, baby. Keep still. It's his head. It's his fucking head.

Cassie You should take him to A and E. If it's his head.

Finn is beginning to calm, beginning to whimper and stop thrashing.
  Eliot examines the injury.

Eliot It's deep, just above his eye.

Cassie I'll call an ambulance.

Eliot No. He's OK.

Cassie They need to check him.

Maggie She's right.

Eliot Just give me the water.

Maggie does.
  Eliot takes it and wets her T-shirt. He dabs at Finn's face, cleaning the blood away.

Cassie He might need stitches. Seriously.

Maggie We could, we could take him.

Eliot No.

Cassie Why?

Eliot We can't, OK? Its complicated, but we can't.

Cassie Your brother's hurt. He needs to go to hospital. I'm calling them.

She reaches for her phone.

Eliot NO!

He grabs it from her.

Maggie Let her.

She tries to grab it off him. He pushes her away.

Eliot You've done enough.

Maggie I'm sorry. I'm really sorry. But we need to take him. Look at him. *Look* at him Eliot. We'll get away with it somehow. We'll say she's on holiday. They won't ask too many questions –

Eliot If some kids came in with a bleeding seven-year-old without a parent in sight I'd ask bloody questions. They'll think we hit him. They'll think – God knows what they'll think –

Maggie Are you blind – none of that matters!

Eliot You don't get it, do you? We're on a register. They told her that. We're already at risk. If any nurse gets a sniff of this and types our names into a computer, we're screwed, we're –

He suddenly realises he may have said too much in front of Cassie.

(*Quieter.*) We're not going.

Maggie I think you're wrong. I'm going to take him.

Eliot Stay away from him.

Maggie You can't stop me.

He takes a step towards her, aggressive.

Eliot I can.

Pause.
Eliot busies himself in tending to Finn.

Cassie Do I call?

Eliot No.

She looks to Maggie for an answer, there is a pause.

Maggie (*quietly*) No.

Cassie takes off her hoodie and gives it to Maggie to put on. She does. She comes to the other end of the table, to her brothers, leaving Cassie at the other end observing, still holding Finn's legs.
Finn is now still, crying softly in gulps.

Maggie I'm so sorry, Finn, I'm so sorry.

Eliot We should get him to count or something. Isn't that what we should do? Get him to count to ten. Count, Finny. Like hide and seek. One. Two . . . Come on. Help me . . .

They both pull him up, leaving Cassie redundant at the other end of the table.

Maggie Come on, Finny. One . . . two.

Finn Three.

Maggie Four.

He starts to cry harder.
Maggie kneels in front of him.

Maggie Five. Come on, baby. Five . . .

Finn (*gulping that turns into a hoarse scream*) My mummy. MUMMY, MUMMY!

Maggie I know you do, baby. I know.

Finn (*a scream that disintegrates into sobs*) MUMMY!

*Maggie tries to pick him up, but can't quite manage it.
Eliot helps and they stand, holding him between them.
All their heads are close. They murmur to him. He
kicks out; they hold him, and soothe him. Cassie can
sense the privacy of the moment, but steals a few
seconds of watching it. Then as Finn begins to calm,
she slowly backs away, takes her bag and makes to
leave. She exits. The door clicks shut.*

    Eliot notices but says nothing.

    *Finn has calmed. They lay him down on the sofa.
They wrap him in a blanket. They cling to each other.
There is a lull.*

Maggie We need to keep him awake, in case . . .

Eliot In case what?

Maggie In case – (*Points to her head and mouths
'concussion'.*)

Eliot With what . . . We can't play music. He'll – (*Points
to the flat above.*) go mental. Maybe we should sing or
something.

    Maggie pauses, then clears her throat.

Maggie Do you remember this from home, Finny, the
one you like . . . The one Mummy would play . . .

    *She hums the first refrain of 'I'm on Fire' by Bruce
Springsteen.*
    Finn shakes his head.

You know it. You told me you liked it. You told me it
was the only one you liked.

    Finn shakes his head.

Fine.

    She sings, imperfectly, a capella, from the first verse.

Finn giggles a little.

You know it don't you . . . yes you do.

Shyly both boys join in.
  Finn laughs.
  As Maggie sings the song, little by little they all join in, imperfectly, like a school assembly.

End of Act One.

Act Two

SCENE FIVE

Eight days later. Nearly midnight.

The room has a twisted domesticity to it now. The children have unpacked a little in a haphazard way, bringing out only the objects they need. We must get the sense that they have really tried to make the place a home, but haven't been sure how. There is evidence that they have all been sleeping in here. The walls are covered with Finn's drawings. The den under the table has been exaggerated with a makeshift flag rigged to the side.

Today is Eliot's birthday. The room has been decorated in cheap party streamers. Eliot, Maggie and Finn sit at the table wearing paper party hats. They are using boxes as chairs. There is an unlit birthday cake in the centre. Finn's cut is now crusty and infected. There is a half-empty bottle of whisky on the table. As the scene begins Eliot pours it sloppily into a paper cup. There is an empty box-chair next to him.

Finn has his head on the table, Maggie stares straight ahead; Eliot looks down at his whisky. They are waiting. We must get the sense they have been waiting a long time. Conversation has been tried, but they have run out of things to say to each other and now sit in silence.

A few moments pass. Eliot pours another drink. Finn kicks the table. Maggie looks at the floor.

There is a knocking at the door. The children look at each other. Another knock. Eliot's face splits into a drunken grin.

Eliot I told you! Didn't I tell you? I told you all.

He stands unsteadily .

Maggie Ellie, the cake you'll knock it –

Eliot No, wait. Let's turn out the lights. Shhh . . .
candles.

*He turns off the lights; Finn is jumping around in
excitement.*
Another knock, Eliot lights the candles.
*They start singing 'Happy Birthday'. Eliot guides
them to the door; Finn's excitement is at fever pitch.
Eliot flings open the door.*
It's Cassie, holding a gift.
Silence. Maggie turns on the lights.

Cassie Happy birthday, Ellie.

Eliot says nothing.

I wanted to drop this off. Sorry I'm so late. I came after
work. I tried calling but . . .

*She holds out her present. He turns his back and walks
away from her.*

Am I interrupting something?

Eliot is trying very hard not to cry.

Finn Can we start the party now?

Eliot Why not? Why the devil not?

*Cassie wanders in. She takes in the state of the room.
It shocks her.*

Finn Can I give you my present now?

Eliot Give the girl a hat.

Finn Presents . . . let's do presents.

Cassie I'm all right, you know.

Maggie forces a hat on her.

Eliot Right then. Party time. Let's play a game or something. Let's just get on with it. If you're late you're late. Eh, Finn . . .

Finn proffers Eliot a very badly wrapped present the size of a shoebox.

Finn Open it! Open it!

Eliot rips the paper off the box and peers inside. He begins to laugh.

Eliot Aw, Finn, you shouldn't have.

Cassie What is it?

Eliot pulls a dead mouse out of the box, holding it by its tail. Both the girls scream.

Eliot Hitler.

Cassie Oh my God, that's disgusting.

Maggie Get rid of it, please get rid of it.

Eliot Finn, you'll go down in history. You killed Hitler.

Finn It's not dead, it's a pet.

Eliot It's pretty much dead, Finn, look.

He swirls the mouse around by the tail. The girls cower.

Finn I put holes in the box and everything.

Eliot But then you wrapped the box.

Finn Oh, yeah.

Maggie Please, please, please get rid of it. I'm begging you.

Cassie I feel sick.

Eliot Ladies . . . ladies, no need to cower, it's only a teeny tiny teeny wee mousey thing. (*He takes a few steps closer, enjoying their fear.*) Look . . .

Finn laughs.

Finn Is it really dead?

Eliot See.

He hands it to him.

Finn I've never seen a dead thing before, it's all hard.

Cassie Eliot, if you don't get rid of that thing I'm going. I mean it.

Eliot grabs the mouse off Finn and puts it back in its box.

Eliot The mouse is back in its house. Coffin closed.

He wipes his hands on his trousers.

Soooo, party time. What do we do now?

Finn Games.

Eliot Right. We've got some age ranges here. But that's OK, I'm down with that. We can find a game for everyone, 'truth or dare' gets a little kinky so let's rule that out.

Finn Kinky, yeah.

Eliot But we can play something nice and fun. Fun for all the family. Something. I don't know. Come on, Finn, you've been to more birthday parties than I have.

Finn Musical chairs.

Eliot We don't have chairs, do we?

Finn Musical boxes.

Eliot Not a real game.

Maggie Musical statues?

Eliot A banger. On the mark, dear Maggie. On the mark indeed. Musical statues. Vintage. Let's do it, but on the condition I, as ringmaster, birthday boy extraordinaire, I make up the rules.

Finn The rules have already been made up, stupid.

Eliot Well, I'm going to change them a little bit, I'm going to jazz them up. That fine by everyone?

He is wild-eyed. They nod.

So. Music.

Finn turns some on. A completely inappropriate tune, it clashes with the atmosphere.

Better music.

Eliot chooses something more dancy.

Now dance.

Eliot switches on a cheap strobe.
   Cassie and Finn dance, Maggie seems unsure.

All of you.

He watches them. Maggie joins in. Finn is a good little groover. His dancing mesmerises them all.

(*To Cassie.*) I taught him that.

In a sudden snap, Eliot turns off the music and the strobe. They freeze in contorted positions. Eliot wanders around them, taking his time.

He or she who moves. Is out. Those are the rules as they stand. But in Eliot's game, Eliot's version if you will . . . the first person that moves has to leave the room. They have to go . . . where do they have to go? Down to the basement perhaps . . . yes, down to the basement. They have to go and wait down there until they are called to rejoin. That is their punishment.

Eliot wanders up to Finn. He blows on his neck. Nothing. He strokes the side of his ribs, Finn giggles, moving.

OUT.

Finn But you're not allowed to –

Eliot It's my game. OUT. Off you go.

Maggie Eliot, that's a bit –

Eliot You playing or not?

Maggie I'm playing.

Eliot Off you go.

Finn But . . .

Eliot You go with him, then.

Maggie Are you serious?

Eliot Fantastically.

Maggie Why the basement?

Eliot You'll see.

Reluctantly they go down.
Eliot waits till he can hear that they are down the stairs then snaps the trapdoor shut and bolts it.

Cassie That's horrible, Eliot.

Eliot You don't have brothers and sisters, do you?

Cassie I don't, but even I know that's cruel –

Eliot You never get a minute to yourself. They always need something. One of them. Always, smelling and climbing all over you. Banging on the door. Even when you're on the fucking bog. Always. They own you. You own each other. There is no such thing as privacy.

Cassie I don't understand –

Eliot Wait till you have a kid. Then you'll know. You can't be yourself around them. Sometimes. It's hard.

Cassie I'm letting them out –

Eliot Don't. Please. Just give me a minute. I just need a minute.

Eliot has walked up to the door. He stands with his back to her. His shoulders shake.

Cassie Are you crying?

Eliot Could you tell me the time, please?

Cassie Almost twelve. Ellie, what's wrong?

Pause. He opens the door. He stares outside.

Eliot Tick-tock. Come on. Come on.

Cassie Who are you waiting for?

Eliot Have you ever wished something so hard it isn't even a wish any more?
Come on. Come on.

Silence.

Come on.

His shoulders shake again.
Cassie creeps up behind him and tries to touch him. He lashes out at her. She backs away, startled.

Eliot Sorry. I. It's not. You. I . . . I . . .
Sorry.
Actually fuck saying sorry. Why is everyone saying sorry the whole time? It's like they can do what they want

and as long as they say sorry it's all right. Like a get-out-of-jail-free card. And it shouldn't work like that. It doesn't work like that.

SOORRRRYYYY.

Means nothing, does it? You can't even hold it. You just say it and it disappears. Poof, into the air.

Cheap word. Cheap words.

He slumps against the wall.

Time please.

Cassie's phone beeps.

Cassie Midnight.

He stares out of the door. He throws his paper hat to the floor.

What's wrong?

He closes the door.

What's going on, Eliot? Talk to me.

Eliot Kiss me. Please.

Cassie Kiss you?

Eliot When you kiss me, this isn't happening. In your mouth there is a place where this isn't happening.

Cassie OK. I can see you're hurt. I can see you're angry. I can see that's something's happened to your mum. But you won't tell me how and you won't tell me why –

Eliot Tell me this isn't happening.

Cassie Why don't you trust me?

Eliot (*singsong*) Ellie the elephant packed his trunk –

Scrabbling can be heard under the door.

Cassie I can hear them, they're trying to get out –

Eliot – and said goodbye to the circus.

Cassie let them out –

Eliot Off he went with a trumpety trump –
   Did your mum ever sing that to you? Or dad. You have a dad, don't you? A dad and a half . . .

Cassie Where's your dad, Eliot?

Eliot Barely remember him. Cancer. Fucking cliché.

Cassie And your mum?

Eliot It should be Nellie the elephant. I only worked that out at school. It was a sad day that. I thought the song was about me.

   Beat.

Nellie the elephant. Ellie the animal. Trapped in your hot car.

Cassie I'm letting them out.

   She tries to open the door. He stands on it.

Eliot Just one more minute.

Cassie Eliot, you're frightening me.

   Pause. She doesn't know what to do. She takes some money from her pocket.

You don't have any. I know you don't have any. Take it. When you let them out, buy them some food. Sober up.

Eliot Don't go. If you go, it starts all over again. Don't go.

Cassie I'm going to put it here.

   She does. Silence. They regard the note between them.

Eliot Don't go.

Cassie Goodnight, Ellie.

Eliot picks up the money. He puts a corner of it in his mouth. Baiting her.

Eliot Delicious.

He puts it in his mouth and chews it.

Like hot chocolate.

Chews more.

Like roast beef . . .

He regards the half-chewed-up note.

Cassie Unbelievable.

Eliot hands the half-note back to her.
  Cassie backs away from his outstretched hand.

I earned that. Do you know what that means? To earn something?

Eliot Have it back.

Cassie backs away further.

Cassie I have a job, after school. A job. Did you know that? No. I forgot. We don't ask each other questions. We just –

Eliot Shhh –

Cassie Fuck you didn't. Like you don't know my surname.
  You've seen where I live. Do you know how hard it is to keep out of trouble there? How hard I work to keep my head above – I'm a novelty to you. My estate's romantic. Flowers out of the pavements. What planet are you on?

Beat.

(*Harder.*) I earned that.
  Unlock your sister.

Eliot looks at her, pleading with his eyes.

Feed her the other half.

Maggie and Finn can be heard shouting to be let out.

Fucking weirdos.

She exits.
Eliot sits alone at the table. The banging increases.
He puts his head in his hands.

SCENE SIX

Ten minutes later.
Maggie is standing covered in dust. Finn stands next to
her, a dark stain on his trousers. He has wet himself.
Eliot is sitting at the table.

Maggie Look at what you've done. Look at him.

She shoves Finn at Eliot.

He's pissed himself. He pissed himself because he was so
frightened.

Beat.

Happy birthday, Eliot.

Eliot Mags, I –

Maggie Just get out. Just go.

Eliot I just needed. I just needed some time. To.

Maggie To what, Ellie? To what? To blow your load?

Eliot Don't.

Maggie Monster.

Eliot Finn, come here.

76

Finn doesn't move.

Finn, I'm sorry. It was a game.

Maggie You think this whole thing is a game, don't you?

Eliot Please try to understand –

Maggie A game where you can play out your little fantasies –

Eliot I needed a few moments, alone, I needed –

Maggie Where you can pretend to be king of your castle –

Eliot I needed time to think –

Maggie And screw your princess while your goblins are locked in the dungeon.
    You just don't think any of this is real, do you? Well, look at him, look at the piss on his trousers. It's real.

Eliot Come here, Finn. I'll change you.

Finn stands behind Maggie.

Finn . . . I'm sorry.

Maggie And what's 'sorry' mean?

Eliot . . . ?

Maggie Nothing, does it?

Eliot We're more alike than you know.

Maggie I am nothing like you. You're like her – your face, your voice, you're like her.

Eliot Don't.

Maggie She who must not be named? Why not? Because the game's up, Ellie. You made sure of that. You just ended it. There's stuff you need to know.

Eliot Not tonight, tonight's not over.

Maggie She missed it. You know she missed it.

Maggie shakes her head, Finn clings to her leg.

Eliot She would never miss it.

Maggie That just proves you never really knew her.

Eliot Right. Let's think. We need to eat. I've got some money. I'm going out to get some food.

Maggie Run, Forest, run.

Eliot I'm going to get us some stuff and we can make a meal and then we'll feel better.

Maggie Coward.

Eliot I am not a coward. I just need some. Air.

Maggie Yeah. We got that.

Eliot I just need some time to think.

Maggie To think what?

Eliot says nothing.

What?

Silence.

That's she's not coming back?

Eliot No.

Maggie That we need help.

Eliot NO.

Maggie Then what? What to make us for dinner? Because if you haven't noticed it's past midnight and things have got a little weird . . . it's time to start facing up to the –

Eliot SHUT UP!

Finn runs from the room.

Maggie I went along with this. I went along with it because I really hoped you were right.

Eliot She could still come, it's not the morning yet.

Maggie Oh Ellie, you've got your face in the stars.

Eliot She could. She could.

Maggie Look at me.

He does.

Eliot, she was a fucking lunatic.

Eliot Don't you dare say that about her –

Maggie She was a fucking head case.

Eliot Shut up –

He comes closer to her.

Maggie A sick, sick woman –

Even closer.

Eliot No.

Maggie She was on shitloads of drugs, Eliot –

Eliot So she takes some medicine, that doesn't make her –

Maggie What do you think those pills were? Maltesers? She was on anti-psychotic drugs.

Eliot No. No. Its not like that, you're making her sound –

Maggie Wake up, Ellie. You need to wake up now. Look at me. She was taking them and she was taking them for a reason, she was not who you think –

Eliot STOP SAYING 'WAS' . . .

Silence.

(*Quieter.*) Don't you dare say 'was'.

I'm going out to get us some food. You watch the phones. We don't want to miss a call. She could have got stuck somewhere.

Maggie We had a deal, Eliot.

Eliot The deal's changed.

Maggie You can't break that promise.

Eliot And we can't break ours.

Maggie I'm calling. I'm calling someone, anyone. This has to end.

He blocks her.

Eliot You promised. We promised. We would stick together. We would stay with Finn. No matter what. If we call someone. We'll be split up. That's what they said. That's what happens. He's too young to stay with us and we're too old for . . . No one will take all three of us. You know that's how it works. It would be hell. Worse than hell. This was her last chance. I can't let you call. I can't. I won't.

Maggie Give me my phone, Eliot. People need to be looking for her now. This is serious.

Eliot She'll come back.

Maggie Give it to me.

Eliot No.

Maggie You can't stop me.

Eliot I have to.

Swiftly he picks up her phone and smashes it. He does the same to his own.

Maggie You bastard. What are we going to do now? What are we going to do?

Eliot We're going to wait, we're going to sit tight –

Maggie You're mad. You've gone mad. You're like her. Can't you see it?

Eliot I'm sorry. But you've just got to trust me. This is for the best –

Maggie You're scaring me. You're scaring me, Ellie.

Eliot I have to do this. It's for our own good. We're not giving up. You hear me?

Maggie backs away from him.

Do you hear me? We're not giving up on her. Because if we do we give up on each other. Understand me?

Maggie stares at him aghast.

I'm going out to get some food. Listen out. She could arrive any minute. Eh?

She won't look at him.

Then we can have a proper party.

He exits, closing the door. Maggie hurls herself against it. She tries to open it and realises its locked. She shouts his name. She sinks to the floor. Finn enters and stares at her. He pads over to her cautiously. She wraps her arms around his waist.

Finn Don't cry.

SCENE SEVEN

Early morning. Maggie is curled up under the table in the den.
Finn is awake, his feet and hands are dirty. He is reading a comic.

There is the sound of the door unlocking. Eliot enters, haggard, having been awake all night. He holds a multipack of crisps. Maggie is awake now, but stays under the table.

Eliot sits at the table, ignoring Maggie.

Eliot Breakfast.

He chucks a packet of crisps at Finn.

Bacon, eh? Close enough.

Finn finds a bowl and pours the crisps in it as if they were cereal. He also puts a bowl on the floor for Maggie.

Finn stares hard at Eliot, chewing his crisps slowly. Pause.

Finn Where did you go?

Eliot To get us food, silly. I hunt, Maggie . . . gathers wood and pebbles and lies. And you, my little squaw, guard the door. Those are the rules.

Finn All night?

Eliot I had to find a special twenty-four-hour shop. It took a long time.

Finn There's one down the road.

Eliot No there is not.

Finn With lights on. There is.

Eliot Well it wasn't open, clever clogs.

Finn It was. I went there.

Eliot You went there?

Finn I was hungry.

Eliot The door was locked.

Finn We have a back door, silly.

Eliot Don't believe you.

Finn They gave me some food and a comic.

Eliot Shut up, Finn, my head hurts.

Finn I didn't have any money. They were nice.

Dawns on him.

Eliot What did you say to them?

Finn That I was hungry.

Eliot What did they ask you?

Finn Stuff. They let me choose whatever comic I wanted. They were really nice.

Eliot Did you go like this? Did you go dirty like this? With no shoes on?

Finn I'd been in the garden – I was trying to bury the rat. So Maggie wouldn't be scared. Then I got hungry.

Eliot This is very important, Finn. What did they ask you?

Finn Stuff. They thought I must be cold with no shoes.

Eliot What did you tell them?

Finn Thank you for the comic and the sandwich.

Eliot Did they ask you about Mummy?

Finn Yes.

Eliot And what did you say?

Finn I'm not stupid.

Eliot What exactly did you say?

Finn That she was asleep at home –

Eliot Thank God.

Finn Under the table.

Eliot Oh my God.

Finn They wanted to take me home and stuff but lots of people came in for beer and I got bored. So I left.

Eliot Did they follow you?

Finn They shouted. But they couldn't see me. I went through the garden.

Eliot And where was Maggie while all of this was going on?

Finn I told you. She was asleep, under the table.

Pause.

Eliot I don't believe you. You're making it up.

Finn Ha ha.

Eliot Hee hee.

Finn Ha ha.

He holds up the comic as if to say 'So there'.

See.

Eliot hits him hard across the face.
  Heavy pause. Finn is gulping. Trying not to cry.

Eliot Eat up.
  These crisps are a treat. When have you ever had crisps for breakfast before?

Finn Mummy –

Eliot Never even made you breakfast.

Beat.

Eat your food.

While all this has been happening Maggie has been opening her crisps as quietly as possible and begun eating them.

Eliot jabs Maggie sharply with his foot.

Eliot Even the dog is eating her breakfast. Go on. Go on.

Finn starts to cry softly.

Don't sit there and cry. You knew not to do that. You knew not to go outside. Stop crying. STOP CRYING!

Maggie Don't –

Eliot She woofs. She woofs and she howls.

Maggie STOP IT!

Finn runs from the room. Brother and sister stare at each other.

It's time.

Maggie goes to open the door.

Eliot Don't.
I'm warning you. Don't open it.

He yanks her roughly away from the door.

Are you mad? Someone will see inside, someone will –

Maggie SOMEONE'S GOT TO SEE, 'CAUSE YOU WON'T.

Eliot Wipe that stuff off.

Maggie Why?

Eliot It's freaking me out. Just take it off.

Maggie Why's it freaking you out, Ellie? 'Cause I look like her? I do, don't I? And you've never liked that. Neither has she.

Eliot Take. Her. Lipstick. Off.

Maggie That's why? Admit it, *it's obvious*.

Eliot Shut up.

He is dangerously close to her now.

Maggie You're more like her than I ever thought. You both can't see the shit from the stars.

Eliot Take that back.

Maggie Like mother, like son. You both only really care about getting laid.

Eliot Bitch.

Maggie Me or her? Because I bet if you blur your eyes you can't tell the difference . . .

Eliot I'm warning you.

Maggie 'Cause you're such a big man now. Aren't you?

She circles him.

Look at him, all tall and proud. He hunts and gathers. He protects –

Eliot Shut your –

Maggie Shimmying through the urban jungle to make a kill. He hunts. He gathers. The man. And he brings back . . . He brings back . . . (*She starts snorting with laughter.*) Crisps . . .

On this last word Eliot gives in, angry. He pounces on his sister, pushing her back onto the sofa. He gets some crisps and rubs them in her face and hair while he has her in a headlock.

Eliot Well, you're fucking eating them, aren't you? Aren't you? AREN'T YOU?

Maggie struggles, feral. Eliot pins her down. She stops struggling. She stares at him.

Would you like some juice to wash that down, madam, freshly made?

Eliot spits on her face.

Completely organic, I assure you.

He sniffs her. He sniffs her again. He picks up her wrists and smells them.

Eliot You put on her perfume.

Maggie Get off me.

Eliot You're dripping in it. Let me smell you.

Maggie You're hurting me.

He lets go.

Eliot Please.

They stare at each other.

Please.

She lets him.

Maggie I was trying to make Finn sleepy. He was so scared last night –

Eliot I hit him. Oh God. I hit him. Maggie –

Maggie It reminded me of when she used to do that. Years ago. She'd spray it on her jumper. When she went out. And we'd sleep with it between us.

Eliot Makes me sleepy too.

Maggie Sleepy boy.

She strokes his hair, he nestles into her.

Tell Mummy where you've been.

Eliot Looking for you.

Maggie That's very sweet of you, but I'm right here.

Eliot You're right here.

Maggie Nothing bad has happened to me.

Eliot Nothing bad.

Maggie Nothing bad at all.

Slowly, throughout this sequence Eliot should get to the point where he's resting his head in her lap.

Where did you look for me?

Eliot By the tracks.

Maggie Did the trains go / choo-choo.

Eliot Choo-choo.

Maggie Did the sirens go / wah-wah.

Eliot Wah-wah.

Maggie Did the doctor go / 'Oh no.'

Eliot 'Oh no.'

Maggie But I wasn't there, was I? I wasn't by the tracks.

Eliot shakes his head.

You didn't even find a piece of skirt.

Eliot I didn't.

Maggie Not one silken clue. Because I just went / poof.

Eliot Poof.

Maggie Off into the air. Without. A. Word.

He turns face up to her.

Eliot Why did you go?

Maggie I'm right here.

Eliot sits up, stares at her hard and hisses.

Eliot Why. Did. You. Go?

Beat.

Maggie Don't be scary, Eliot, it doesn't suit you.

Eliot Tell me why.

Maggie You have crisps on your face.

Eliot Fuck you.

Maggie I wish you'd fuck something, then maybe you'd concentrate, even a tiny bit, on the enormous, gargantuan, motherfucking problem we've got on our hands.

Beat.

No pun intended.

Eliot I am concentrating on it.

Maggie We're a mess, Eliot. Look at us.

Eliot We're OK.

Maggie shakes her head.

We are, we are . . .

Maggie When I went to get her perfume. I stood in her clothes. I went and stood in her clothes. Just stood there, swaying with them.

She grabs Eliot, turning him to face her, desperate now.

Eliot Please don't –

Maggie Just to be close to something that hung on a clothes hanger like a body, the same shape as her body, and then I started to think of bodies hanging and then I . . .

She lets go of him.

It's like a ghost story without a ghost.

Eliot It's your imagination. Rein it back. Rein it back.

Finn peeks out cautiously.

Maggie (*echoes*) Rein it back.

Finn Just like a horse.

Maggie Just like a horse.

He sits in her lap.

Eliot We just have to wait.

Maggie I can't wait any longer. Look at me, I can't. We can't.

Eliot She's done this before.

Maggie Never like this and you know it.

Finn She's right.

Eliot Come on, troops. This isn't the spirit. Let's take check. Finn Bar, slightly ruffled but still in fighting form, Maggie, could do with a proper night's sleep, but otherwise we're OK, aren't we? We've still got some money –

Maggie How much?

Eliot Some. Enough.

Maggie How much exactly?

Eliot Thirty quid?

Maggie Thirty quid? We had two hundred. I knew you'd do this. I knew it. I should have hidden it better. I should have –

Eliot Well, we had those takeaways and the cider and we bought the strobe –

Maggie What are you? Harry fucking Potter? You gonna magic some more? Thirty quid. That's nothing. *Nothing.*

Eliot It's not nothing –

Finn You spent our money?

Maggie I bet you spent it on her, didn't you? I bet you spent *our* money. *Our* food money on getting her pissed.

Eliot Leave her out of it.

Finn Stop it.

Maggie I wish *you'd* leave her out of it. Acne Romeo. Sniffing around her. Sweating. Plying her with warm cider. Just have a wank. It's cheaper.

Eliot Don't be disgusting.

Maggie Disgusting? You're the disgusting one. A spineless panting bag of hormones. Where's my big brother? Who's always been taller than me? Who's always led the way? Remember when she left us in the car. By the supermarket. When she wandered off. And it was so hot and Finn started to cry. And the door was locked and she didn't come back for hours. Remember that? How you made it into a game and made it go away and how it was you, always you . . . My brother, trapped in a hot car with a face like the sun. My brother. King of my childhood. Where the fuck are you? (*A harsh whisper.*) Are you gone too?

Pause. Her words hang in the air. She has said the unspoken.

Maggie We were always afraid of this. Always. All those nights. The time she actually tried.

Eliot She got carried away, it was an accident, she didn't really mean to –

Maggie You believe that? You still believe that? She said that stuff to make you feel better, Ellie –

Eliot It was the truth –

Maggie All the banging we did with pots and pans to keep her awake until the ambulance came.

Eliot That was years ago, she was getting better.

Maggie Don't you remember the sound?

Finn bangs.

Bang, bang. Bang. Throwing water on her. Are you conveniently forgetting that – ?

Eliot She was so much better. Things had changed –

Finn Bang bang bang –

Maggie Because it seems like you're forgetting, it seems like you're remembering someone different, it seems like we have different –

Finn Bang bang bang.

Eliot STOP IT! ALL OF YOU STOP IT!

Finn runs to his den.

Maggie You're not listening to me. You stopped listening to me a long time ago.

Eliot What are you saying we do? (*Lowered voice.*) We'll get farmed off to some teenage care home, some practice flat, and they will put Finn in separate foster care before his feet touch the linoleum. She had one last chance –

Maggie And she ruined it, Eliot.

Eliot Not yet. I believe in her, OK? I believe in her.

Maggie That's not enough. Belief is not enough. It's time to wake up.

She stands up. He pushes her down roughly.

Eliot (*frightening*) NO! We will wait here. Until we are starving. Until we can't handle a moment more of it. Because if we give in, we are basically surrendering our little brother to strangers. He'll grow up without us.
Do you understand me?

Maggie nods.

We have no choice but to wait, we have no choice but to hope. Because that is what family is. Suffering for each other. Suffering each other.

Maggie Jesus Christ.

Eliot Exactly.

A new mobile phone begins to ring. It is neither of theirs. The sound is coming from the den.

Where is that coming from?

More ringing.

What the . . .

Maggie and Eliot scan the room for the sound. They pounce on the den. Ripping it apart. They find Finn in the centre, hands over his head with a mobile phone flashing next to him.

That's her phone. Eliot! That's her phone.

Eliot snatches it. The ringing finishes. He holds it as if it is on fire.

Where did you find this?

Finn whimpers.

WHERE?

Maggie This is very important, Finny, tell us where you found it . . .

Finn In a box.

Maggie Why didn't you tell us?

Finn I thought it was a toy 'cause it didn't work. Then I plugged it in.

Eliot lays the phone down on the table. They all stand around it.

Maggie Ring the number back. Do it.

Eliot I am. I will. Just. Let's think for a minute. If she left the phone, that would explain why she hasn't called. Why it was off. Because she probably doesn't know our numbers –

Maggie I'm done with thinking. I'm done with it –

She tries to snatch the phone. Eliot stops her.

Finn Is it really Mummy's phone?

Maggie Look at it.

Finn Well then, it can't be her. Why would she call her own phone? Stupid.

*There is a beep. The number has left a message.
Eliot is staring hard at the phone.*

Maggie They've left a message. Get the message. It could be news.

Eliot calls.

What is it?

Eliot There's a few from us. Wait.

Maggie Put it on loudspeaker.

He does. We hear the first few seconds of Finn's last message to her. Eliot deletes it. Then we hear the message just left.

Katie (*voice-over*) Claire darling, it's Katie. Look, Roland and I feel terrible. We wanted to come round sooner but we've been stuck up with my parents. Mum had a hip replacement. Complete nightmare. We've only just got back to town. We've been trying you all week. Did you get our card? I put our number. Anyway, listen, we're going to pop round in about half an hour, got something we want to drop off. I hope we catch you. And hon, I hope you're feeling better. You were quite wobbly when you came round. Scared us a little if I'm honest. But I'm sure you're fine. Moving is so stressful. Gets to the best of us. (*Nervous laugh.*) Anyway, darling. We'll see you later. Love to the kids. Bye.

Eliot Shit.

Maggie It's over.

Eliot No it's not. Let me think.

Maggie It is, Ellie. They're coming round. They'll smell something's up in a second. You heard her. They're obviously worried –

Eliot Shut up. Let me think.

Maggie You can't stop them coming here. You can't stop me telling them. It's over, Eliot. It's too serious now.

Eliot We could pretend we're not in. That'll buy us some time.

Maggie Do you not get it? I'm not doing this any more, Eliot. I'm telling them the truth.

Eliot We can just turn off the lights. They'll think we're out.

Maggie Would you listen to me? You can't stop me.

Beat.

Why are you looking at me like that?

Eliot I'm sorry.

Maggie Why . . . Why, Eliot?

Eliot Just know I'm sorry.

Blackout.

SCENE EIGHT

The flat. Half an hour later. Finn is alone in the room.
He is trying to get the last crumbs out of the empty crisp
packets. Unsatisfied, he searches the cupboards, the fridge.
There is only one tin of golden syrup. He cannot open it.
There is a knock on the door.
Another knock.

Katie (*offstage*) Claire. CLAIRE? Hello?

More knocking. Finn ignores it, still struggling with
the tin.

Roland (*offstage*) She must be out. We can leave it on
the doorstep.

Katie (*offstage*) In this area? Are you mad? Besides, the
chocolate will melt.

On the word 'chocolate' Finn runs to the door and
opens it. Revealing Katie and Roland. A couple in
their forties, they are expensively dressed, crisp smart
casual. Roland is holding a gift hamper. A box of
chocolates sits on the top.

Katie Finn. Darling. We didn't think you were in. We
were just about to –

Finn silently yanks at the hamper, dragging Roland into the room. Katie follows. They are shocked by the state of the room.

Roland Jesus.

Katie Finn, where is everyone?

Finn ignores her, ripping at the chocolate.

Roland Look at this place. The smell.

Katie Darling, look at me? Are you here on your own?

Finn shakes his head.

Hello? Anyone at home? Claire?
Where is everyone?

Finn points to the floor.

What do you mean? What does he mean?

Suddenly Eliot pops out of the trapdoor covered in dust. He holds a roll of industrial tape. Panic flashes across his face. He quickly composes himself.

Eliot Roland. Katie. What a wonderful surprise.

Katie I could say the same. Just popping up like that. We were starting to think Finn was here on his own. Little mite.

Eliot Of course not. I was just . . . doing some . . . work in the basement. Maggie and Mum are at the shops, aren't they, Finn? So I . . . we thought we'd have some boy time. Finn was on a break, weren't you? Tiring work.

He is breathing hard.

Roland Are you converting it? The basement.

Eliot Yes sirree. How did you get in?

Katie Finn let us in –

Eliot I thought I told you never to answer the door to strangers, Finn? Didn't I tell you that?

Katie We're not strangers, though, are we?

Eliot No. You're not. Well. Lovely of you to drop by –

Katie I must say. We're relieved to hear your mum is out and about. She was a bit wobbly when she came round. Wasn't she, Roland?

Roland A bit tearful.

Eliot When was that?

Katie The day after you moved. Poor thing. Moving just sucks the life out of you. And with three kids. I'm not surprised she's having the odd cry. I mean. We've been redecorating and that's more than enough, isn't it, Roland?

Roland Quite.

Katie I mean, if you're renovating as well. Poor woman. Are you sure she's all right? We sent her that card and left a ton of messages. We just feel. You know. It can be lonely, this city, it can get you down, so –

Eliot She's on top form, really. Smashing. Tell them, Finn.

Finn All cool, yeah.

Katie Are you sure though? Look at this place.

Roland Katie –

Katie I'm sorry, Roland, but it's a bit of a state, are you sure she's coping –?

Eliot No no. She is. This place. It's a mess because. Well, we only moved in a week ago and . . .

He spies a bit of wilting party décor and grabs it.

We had a party, didn't we, Finn?

Finn Kinky, yeah.

Roland What did he say?

Eliot Ignore him. Yes. It was my birthday. It got a bit out of hand.

Katie Teenagers. No wonder she's gone out. You'd better get this place sorted before –

Finn, having gorged on the chocolate, attacks the hamper, feral, thirsty.

Darling, that's a present, it's all arranged, really. Stop it now.

Finn JUICE!

Katie What do you say?

Finn Juice, please.

Eliot Finn, behave.

Katie rifles in the hamper.

Katie No no. It's fine. As it happens. We had some wine, didn't we, Roland? And then, well, we thought. Soft drinks would probably be more. With your mum. You know. So we stopped at a petrol station. They didn't have anything fresh so –

She pulls out a Ribena.

But there were just so many kinds. I didn't know which one you would like so I thought. You only live once –

She unloads every available type of Ribena onto the table.

I got them all.

Finn attacks a carton.

Do you like the Ribena, sweetie? Is it tasty?

Finn spits some onto the floor.

Eliot You little fucking moron.

Heavy reproach of his swearing can be heard in the air.

Sorry. I'm just a bit. Stressed at the moment. With the move and cleaning up. You know. The party. We had a late night. Sorry, Finn.

Katie Well you really should clear this up before she gets back –

Eliot We will –

Katie Not that we can talk. We just had the builders in and it was a complete nightmare. I mean you wouldn't believe the mess people make. We had a skylight put in and –

Eliot A skylight? That's wonderful, but we really should be getting on, so thanks for –

Katie You could do with a skylight in here. But there's a flat above, isn't there? We thought you had the whole house. But I suppose with the property market the way it is. Anyway. A bit of extra light can do wonders. For the mind, you know. It can really change the way a room feels –

Roland Katie got into her Zen thing.

Katie You mustn't call it that.

Roland She started going to these classes in Earl's Court.

Katie Hatha yoga.

Roland And suddenly the house had to be –

Katie He just wriggled and writhed, but we just had to make the change. We even have a gym because Roland's heart –

Roland My heart is fine.

Katie You've got to watch the salt in your diet, even at your age, Eliot, it sneaks up on you –

Roland Will you tell your mum we stopped by?

Eliot Of course.

Katie Tell her we're here any time. Say goodbye, Finn. God, look. He's got chocolate all over his face, I think I've got a tissue somewhere . . .

She grabs tissues from her bag and starts daubing at Finn's face. She spies the cut. It is now crusty and infected.

Roland Look after yourself. Give us a call if you need a good builder. Although ours are complete pirates –

She touches it lightly, Finn yelps.

Katie How did he get this cut, Eliot –?

Eliot Climbing frame –

Katie It doesn't look good. Keep still, darling. Let me see. I think it's infected. Where does your mother keep the first-aid kit?

The boys stare at her blankly.

Has Claire seen this? It looks old. I mean. I'm no nurse but this looks like it should have had stitches. Keep still, darling.

Roland Isn't there one in the –?

Katie The boot. Yes. Come on, Finn. Let's get a look at this in the light.

They leave. Roland seems about to follow but hesitates at the doorway. He turns back round. Eliot stares at him. Hard. Roland closes the door a little.

Roland Is she really all right, Eliot?

Eliot What do you want?

Roland You can tell me.

Eliot Fuck off.

Roland What?

Eliot You heard me. Fuck. Off.

Roland That's no way to speak to –

Eliot To what?

Roland An adult.

Eliot I prefer the term cuckolding-dick-fuck, but if we're going to split hairs . . .

Roland Eliot –

Eliot Oh. I'm sorry. Does your wife not know you've been fucking my mother?

Small pause.

Of course not.

Roland Look. I'm not going to lie to you, Eliot. There was something, yes. But it's over. It finished over six months ago –

Eliot Bullshit. You led her on. All those weekends. She came back smelling of you, for Christ sakes. Smelling of you and cheap hotels. Or were the hotels nice? Was she worth a champagne breakfast?

Roland You've got this wrong –

Eliot Skating a bit close to the bone, aren't you? Coming here together? Very modern of you, though, very modern indeed –

Roland She's a family friend. We both know her. We both care.

Eliot Don't insult me, you never gave a fuck –

Roland That's not true.

Eliot Just get out.

Roland Listen to me. I did care. I do care. And I'll be frank –

Eliot You've got five seconds to get your scraggy white shitty –

Roland LISTEN for Christ sake. When she came round. Look, she was as bad as I'd ever seen her, Eliot. And look at the state of Finn. So let's cut the crap. Tell me the truth –

Eliot For the love of God. She's fine. Finn's fine. It's a cut, OK? Kids get cuts –

Roland Then why hasn't she returned our calls?

Eliot Because she doesn't want to see you? Because you broke her heart, because you made promise after promise then dumped her like a stray dog –

Roland She was deluded. She believed what she wanted to believe. Eliot, she was depressed –

Eliot GET OUT GET OUT GET OUT.

Roland Oh Eliot. I want to help.

A smash from the basement.

What was that?

Eliot Nothing.

Another smash.

They're building next door, all right? Adding forty-five skylights or some shit. Now GET OUT!

Roland Let me help.

Eliot If you don't fuck off this instant I will scream so loudly your balls will curdle. I will shout until Katie rushes back in here, probably because it sounds like you are raping me, then I will tell her every sick fucking detail about your affair –

Roland Oh for God's sake, Eliot, grow up –

Eliot Don't believe me? Fine. KATIIIEE . . .

Roland Just think for a minute. Just think about Claire, Katie is her only friend in London, do you really think telling her is –

Eliot I will bomb Katie with every detail. The hotels you went to. Your craggy hand on her head, her back, her arse. I'll tell her everything. 'Cause you know what, Rollo? Favoured son knows all.

Pause.

Go on. Go. Don't pretend we ever meant anything to you.

Roland You're serious, aren't you?

Eliot Deadly.

They stare at each other.

Now get out. Gucci pig.

Roland sighs.

You know where we are.

He goes to the door. He swings it open to reveal Maggie covered in dust. Her hand is bleeding.

Maggie? What the . . .

Maggie stands silent in the doorway. Suddenly she springs at Eliot, lashing, scratching. Blood gets on his face.

STOP IT!

He pulls her off.

Jesus. Maggie. Your hand. What happened to your hand?

Maggie struggles in his arms. Eliot backs away.

Maggie I will never forgive you. I will *never* forgive you.

Roland What's happened?

Maggie He locked me. He locked me down there. But I got out. I broke the window and I got out.

Eliot It was a game.

Roland It doesn't look like a game to me.

Eliot Go. This is between us. Just leave.

Maggie How could you do that to me? How could you?

Roland What happened, Maggie? He said you were with –

Eliot I'LL TELL KATIE. I'LL SCREAM IT IN HER EAR!

Roland You think I'm going now –

Eliot I'll do it. I will.

Pause.

Roland Tell her. Tell her everything. I'm not going anywhere. Hear me? I'm calling your mother. I'm –

He calls.

Eliot Don't.

Katie enters.
   The phone rings on the table. Eliot slams it off.

Katie Maggie?

Roland That's her phone.

Eliot And how would you know that?

Katie I heard shouting. From across the street. I left your brother in the car. He told me some very worrying things, he said he's been sleeping on the floor. Where's Claire? Did she come back with Maggie? Where is she?

Maggie Don't you get it? We don't know where she is.

Eliot Don't, Maggie. Don't.

Maggie She's missing.

Katie Since when?

Maggie The day after we got here.

   Eliot turns his back. He is trying desperately to think of something.

Roland That's over a week ago –

Katie You haven't heard from her? Nothing?

   Maggie shakes her head.

Roland And you've been on your own?

   Maggie nods.

Katie Oh, Maggie. Oh, sweetheart.

   Maggie crumbles. Katie goes to her.

I think we should call the police.

   Roland nods. Eliot, desperate, blocks the door.

Eliot NO, you've done enough to us. Enough.

Katie This is serious now, Eliot –

Eliot Don't you see? This is his fault. HIS FAULT. It all makes sense now.

He is dangerously close to Roland.

Eliot You were the last person to see her. It was that day. That same day. What did you say to her, Roland? What did you say to make her run away?

Katie She came to see us both, Eliot, we –

Eliot You believe that?

Roland Don't do this –

Eliot Let the wild rumpus start!

Katie What does he mean? Roland?

Eliot What came out of your cunting mouth? I WANT TO KNOW!

Katie What is he talking about?

Eliot That she was too crazy for you, that she had too much lipstick on her teeth –?

Roland I would never hurt –

Eliot You led her on, didn't you? She told me everything. Everything. Who do you think she whispered to? Maggie? She never was a girly girl. It was me. I put my ear against her stories and I heard. You and the ocean roaring in pleasure . . .

He takes a step closer.

Eliot You told her that your marriage was dead. That you were just waiting for the right time. And she believed you. She moved down to London to be nearer you. You told her that to fuck her, didn't you? DIDN'T YOU?

Roland It wasn't like that –

Eliot Liar, liar!

Roland I promise you –

Eliot Pants on fucking fire!

Roland Look. I. It was –

Eliot Tell me the truth.

Katie Answer him.

Eliot THE TRUTH!

Roland I –

Eliot steps closer.
He pauses. He looks at Katie.

Katie Go on.

Roland I loved your mother.

Katie makes a sound of pain.

Eliot That's not enough. Answer my fucking question, what did you say?

Roland I told her . . . Christ!

He looks at Katie, who has turned away from him.

I told her it was over for good.

Eliot You. I see it now. I see everything. It's your fault. It's his fault. You used her. Blood on your hands. Blood in your mouth. You cunt. Hell would be a holiday for you.

Maggie You're wrong, Eliot. So wrong.

Eliot Maggie, it was him. He was the last person to see her –

Maggie Fools. What a joke. Look at you. Joke on you both!

Eliot Can't you see? It was him.

Maggie It was me.

Small pause.

Eliot I don't believe you. You would have said, you would have –

Maggie Said? You're the one that does the saying, Eliot. You've had your say this whole rancid time, haven't you? You've done what you wanted and I've let you. So sit tight for once in your life and fucking listen to me.

Eliot What the fuck are you talking about?

Maggie Once upon a time, there was a family. One mummy bear, two baby boy bears and a girl cub. And the mother seemed to hate the daughter yet love her two boys very much.

It was a strange family. Because the thing is, Mummy Bear was sick. But she didn't want to frighten her darling boy cubs. But the girl cub, well, scaring her she didn't mind so much. Who knows why, but Mummy didn't like girl cubs. They saw right through her. They weren't made dozy with her charms. And Mummy Bear didn't like that. She liked her charms, she did. They were all she had left.

Time passed and the poorly Mummy Bear started coming to the girl cub in the middle of the night, pregnant with dark secrets. She would share them with the girl and they would lie together, spooning in the dark . . . and in those few poisonous hours they would be close because . . . because . . . what brings you closer than sharing hell –

Eliot Don't, please, don't –

Maggie So the girl bear would walk her around night after night when she couldn't sleep and it was her, only her who would change her mummy bear's clothes when she was too low to even move and it was only this girl, this girl cub, who knew she tried it twice. Then three times, but I sorted her out, I helped her be sick and we never told anyone. *Anyone.* It was our secret –

Eliot That's not true –

Maggie Our black secret.

Eliot You're lying. She didn't, she was getting better –

Maggie She was getting worse and you slept your way through it –

Eliot No.

Maggie You don't know. It was me who listened. It was me who held her and listened. Her sour breath on my face.

Roland Christ.

Eliot Stop it stop it stop it.

Maggie I was the last person to see her. It wasn't him. It was me. I never told you that. I wanted to so many times. So many times, Eliot. But I couldn't, you had your face so firmly in the fucking stars I couldn't tell you what I said to her, I couldn't. I kept waiting for you to be my big brother and take me in your arms and ask what was wrong. Because I thought it was written on my face so bright it could have been lipstick.

Eliot What did you say? What did you say to her . . .

Small pause.

Maggie Something inside me just . . . I just knew it would be like every other time. Over and over. And I was so angry. So fucking angry with her. My tummy hurt and

I couldn't even tell her. She was crying again. Walking in circles. I tried to make her something to eat. You two were at the park. She shoved it out of my hand. She told me I was an accident. A piece of shit like my dead father. The same old routine. She started crying again. And it was like she couldn't see me. I was begging her to calm down, to pull herself together. And it was like she couldn't see me. And she started threatening things. You know. What she would do . . .

Eliot What did you say to her?

Maggie I said . . .

  Beat.

'Just go and do it then.'

  Silence.
  Maggie crumples.

I ran out of the house. I got to the park and I watched you. For a bit, before you saw me. And I was going to tell you. I wanted to tell you everything. But you looked so happy. Playing in the sun. I couldn't. I just couldn't. So I pretended nothing had happened. And when we got back she was gone.

Eliot No.

Maggie She was different to you, Eliot. She thought the sun shone out of your mouth. She worshipped you. She protected you from it. From the worst bits, and so did I –

Eliot Please tell me you're lying.

  Maggie shakes her head.

Maggie I told her to do it and she has. She has.

Eliot Please . . .

  She shakes her head.

Roland goes to Katie, to put a hand on her shoulder.

Roland We should call.

Katie Don't touch me.

Roland Katie, I . . .

She shakes her head. She goes over to Maggie.

Your hand. You need a plaster. You need.
  It's not your fault. You know that, sweetheart? Never think it's your fault. You have both been so brave.

Maggie clings to her hand.

I'm going to go outside now. I'm going to call the police. People need to be looking for her. OK? We still don't know what's happened. OK. But we're going to find out, sweetheart . . . Now let go.

Maggie keeps clinging.

You're going to stay with us tonight. You're all going to stay with us for as long as it takes. I'll look after you. I promise. We can even go shopping. Proper shopping.
  Just wait in here. The phone call shouldn't take too long. Maybe pack a few things. I'll get Finn.

She exits.
    After a second Roland follows.
    Finn wanders sleepily through the door.

Finn Maggie! You're out!
  I fell asleep in the car. I had my sailing dream again.

Maggie Where were you sailing?

Finn It was all of us.

Sounds of a muffled argument can be heard A loud slam. A sob. Finn peeks through the peephole.

I didn't like him. She was nice, though. Ooo, they're fighting. She hit him with her bag.

Maggie and Eliot look at each other. For the first time since she told him. They stare at each other. Eliot comes to her. He seems about to say something but can't.

She hit him again! Hard.

Maggie Tell us more about your dream, Finn.

Finn I told you. It was just us. In the boat.

Maggie Made of golden-syrup cans?

Finn Of course.

Eliot spies Roland's jacket. He slips his hand inside and takes out a wallet.

Maggie What are you doing?

Eliot has slipped out a sheaf of notes and two cards.

Eliot Was it an adventure?

Finn I would say so. Yes.

Maggie Eliot, put that back.

Eliot We're going to need it . . . what are they doing, Finn?

Finn checks.

Finn He's crying. She's . . . she still looks mad.

Eliot Then we've got time.

He shoves some belongings into a bag.

Maggie What are you talking about?

Eliot We can get out through the garden.

Maggie No.

Eliot I'll carry Finn. Come on. Quickly.

Maggie shakes her head.

They will separate us. You know that.

Maggie I'm tired, Eliot. I'm so tired –

Eliot Get up.

He looks at the door.

We have a few minutes . . . if that . . . Come on.

She doesn't move. He kneels down by her.

If they come back in and we're still here it's all over.
Understand that. All over. Even if Mum does come back.
The game's up.

Maggie Where will we go?

Eliot To Brighton, Stonehenge, Land's End, anywhere . . .
We could just take a train . . . We've got some money
now. We'll be together. We'll be all right.

Maggie shakes her head.

We will. Somehow. We'll figure it out. But anything.
Listen to me, *anything* is better than what's about to
happen if we stay here. We have to try.

Maggie No.

Eliot (*urgent*) Other people's hands putting him to bed at
night, other people's hands all over him. Our brother.
We swore we would never let it happen. We promised.
Get up. Come on. Don't fall now.

Get up.

Beat.

Get up.

He drags her up.

You wanted your big brother and here I am. I'm just
telling you what we have to do. I'm leading the way.
There's nothing for us here. Just follow me.

Maggie Do you forgive me?

Their eyes meet.

Eliot Do you forgive me?

A pause. She nods sadly.

Then follow me.

Eliot exits.
Finn looks around the room. Torn.

Maggie You can stay if you want and I'll stay too.

*Finn takes a final look around the room. He is small,
unsure.*
*They hear a call. The same call Eliot used at the
beginning. Red Indian. Tribal. Finn listens. Finn calls
back. He looks at Maggie. He nods. She nods.*
Slowly, they follow Eliot into the light.

The End.